3—

D0897590

THE LAST DRAGON OF STEEPLE MORDEN

THE LAST DRAGON OF
STEEPLE MORDEN

To Robert
All the Best.
Enjoy!
John Kevil

To Robert
My Best!
Bill Fullerton

JOHN J. KEVIL, JR.

authorHOUSE®

AuthorHouse™
1663 Liberty Drive
Bloomington, IN 47403
www.authorhouse.com
Phone: 1-800-839-8640

Published by AuthorHouse   06/05/2012

ISBN: 978-1-4685-6246-0 (sc)
ISBN: 978-1-4685-6426-6 (hc)
ISBN: 978-1-4685-9686-1 (e)

Library of Congress Control Number: 2012907437

for Bill Cullerton and all Allied Fighter Pilots of World War II

Contents

II

Introduction

Sometimes a story of solitary human endeavor must be told. We need to hear stories about people who take chances, who step in and out of character to reveal their inner strengths. Their extraordinary human intrigues raise the bar on the will to survive. At the very least, a story can pay homage to someone who deserves the legacy. Lastly, a story stares you in the face and it must be told simply because it is so fantastic.

The World War II (WWII) story that follows is both fantastic and true. It is a story of love and honor, heroism and horror, and of the strength of the mind to survive when the rules of nature emphatically declare that it is time to die. I first heard this story as a child, and I have acquired much more information over the course of forty years. I have always felt that this amazing story, which is well understood and appreciated by those close to the Cullerton family, has never been fully grasped by many people who have heard only pieces of it.

WWII was a different time. By the time of America's involvement in WWII, most Americans were united in the cause. Mothers waited for their sons, wives waited for their husbands, and fiancés waited for their betrothed to return. As men went to fight on two foreign fronts, women worked to build the machinery for war. Britain had been doing the same thing for more than two years by the time

America joined the war. Four hundred thousand American soldiers, sailors, and marines died in faraway places. This means that nearly ten thousand Americans died every month during America's forty-two month involvement in WWII. These terribly high numbers are staggering when compared to all conflicts the United States has engaged in since. Over the span of seventy years since WWII began, America has lost approximately one hundred twenty thousand soldiers. Yet the American casualties are small in comparison to the total deaths worldwide at the end of the War in 1945. The Second World War of the twentieth century claimed fifty-five million people globally, more than twice the number of deaths attributed to World War I, and by all accounts, Bill Cullerton should have been one of those 55 million casualties.

Near Ansbach, Germany

It is the last month of the war in Europe, and fighter squadron elements of the 355th Fighter Group out of Steeple Morden, England, are patrolling German skies near Ansbach, Germany, looking for German airfields and anything related to the German military. Four Mustangs of the 357th Squadron have spotted a German airfield below.

**SCHEMATIC REFERENCE MAP OF
GERMANY DURING WORLD WAR II**

△ HILLS   ⋀ MOUNTAINS   🌲 FOREST

The Strafing Pass

April 8, 1945

The four Mustangs spotted the German aerodrome ahead; the runways were lined with German fighter planes. Flight leader Captain Bill Cullerton barked out the attack plan as the four American P-51D Mustangs zeroed in for a strafing attack.

"Weideman and I will make the first pass north to south; Garlich, you guys follow, east to west."

"Roger that, Flight Leader." With that, Cullerton and Weideman nosed their Mustangs down, leveling off at forty feet above the ground, traveling at two hundred miles an hour. Their combined twelve .50 caliber, wing-mounted, machine guns began to strafe the German aircraft on the runway. Bill destroyed one plane, sent a second one into flames, and then a third—and that's when it happened. Cullerton's plane bucked; it had taken a direct hit in the fuselage, right behind the pilot's seat, from a twenty millimeter German anti-aircraft cannon concealed in the trees. Cullerton's plane exploded, and his wingman, Lieutenant Bob Weideman, was hit by machine gun fire as well. Weideman's plane was damaged but still airworthy for the moment. Weideman requested permission to get his damaged plane out of Germany to somewhere safe. He broke off and tried to nurse his plane to France. As Lieutenant Garlich began his own strafing pass, he heard the explosion and looked over to see Cullerton's plane erupt with flames. Garlich pulled up as he took several machine gun hits; he was losing fuel. He couldn't see Cullerton's plane when he looked around again, only a fireball. Cullerton was gone. Garlich couldn't believe it. He had seen yet another Steeple Morden strafer killed in action.

I

The West Side of Chicago

December 5, 1941

Bill Cullerton awoke with a start and sat bolt upright in bed. His hands instinctively pushed his long coal-colored hair back out of his face. He tried to regain focus as he looked around his bedroom; he was freezing. He looked down and saw that he was sleeping only in his underwear, again. His head ached and his eyes strained to focus. He noticed that his window was wide open and his blanket was nowhere to be found. Bill had been sabotaged. There was only one person who would try to freeze him out: his mother, Ethel. His sister, Jean, wasn't capable of this sort of treachery. "Real funny, Mom!" Cullerton exclaimed. If freezing his ass off in his own bed wasn't bad enough, his headache was intensifying. He wondered if he might still be drunk from the night before.

To make matters worse for Bill, as he was lying in bed and still coming out of his cold confusion, the wind-up alarm clock began to blare. The tattletale copper clock was not where it was supposed to be; it was way the hell across the room on top of his highboy dresser. "Thanks, Mom," he yelled as he rolled out of bed.

It was 6:30 a.m., and Bill had already taken a good measure of abuse. He looked at the open window, "No sense in wasting this open window," he muttered to himself as he pulled out a book of matches and a Chesterfield cigarette, filterless of course, from the top drawer of his dresser. Bill leaned on the window frame and looked out over the Austin neighborhood, located on the far west side of Chicago. As he puffed away, he could see the bruises beginning to surface over his beat-up body. He glared back at the clock; he had gotten only two hours and ten minutes of sleep. Doing a quick mental tally, Bill figured he'd had about nineteen hours of sleep over the last several days.

Bill had graduated high school six months earlier and had been living the life ever since. A typical evening consisted of getting off work or finishing class at Wright City College, followed by football practice (semipro), going out to dinner or a movie with the girlfriend, Elaine, and getting her home to Oak Park no later than midnight. After that, it was back to the city to drink and party with friends until four or five in the morning. Somehow, Bill would drive or take the el home, sleep until ten, and repeat the cycle. So far it was working out pretty well for him, but he could never figure out why the midnight to 5:00 a.m. part of the night went by so fast.

Bill had had a passable fake ID since August. His buddy worked at the post office in Chicago's Austin District and had "procured" a fake federal ID for him. A lot of guys had the standard altered driver's license, but very few had a fake federal ID. These days, though, Bill only needed the ID to get into the afterhours joints, where he had already made a lot of friends.

Since Bill was a semipro football player in Chicago, drinking wasn't an option, it was a requirement. The guy who owned Bill's team, the Austin Bears, also owned a tavern. In the CFL (Chicagoland Football League), owning a tavern was a requirement for team owners, because most players got paid in beer and pretzels. Besides, a neighborhood bar was a great place to promote a team.

Bill continued to stare out the open window. He was in hot water with his mother and his girlfriend on a regular basis these days. He knew he had been pushing his luck for a while, but he didn't have any plans to revise his current routine; he was having too good a time to want to make any changes. He didn't see his dad, Orville, too often, and that was fine; they weren't getting along too well these days, anyway.

His mother's early morning sleep sabotage had a couple of reasons behind it: retribution, for coming home at 4:00 a.m., and getting Bill's butt out of bed so he could pick up Elaine and drop her off to school on time. "Damn," he said out loud as looked at the clock again and then quickly started to get ready. Bill was alone in the house; his mother had taken his sister, Jean, to school. She attended Trinity High, an all-girls' high school in nearby River Forest.

Bill ran out of the house, jumped into his Ford "bathtub" convertible, and headed to Oak Park to pick up Elaine and drive her to Rosary College, a women's college, also in River Forest. He headed south to Madison Avenue and then turned west to Oak Park. The stoplights were in his favor today; it looked as though he'd make it to Elaine's on time.

Elaine Stephens, "Steve" to her friends, was Bill's girl. "Steve" was an odd nickname for a girl who had been considered the prettiest girl in her class at Trinity (class of '41), but Bill had been calling her "Steve" the two years they had been dating, so everyone else had started using it too.

Bill arrived at Steve's house on Wesley Avenue at 7:30 sharp and honked. Steve's mother waved from the doorway; Bill smiled and waved back. Steve was always very prompt, so he waited in the car . . . and waited . . . and waited some more. *Hmm. She must be running late,* he thought to himself.

As he waited, Bill stared at the porch and remembered a date they had gone on a year ago. His football team at Fenwick Catholic had won that day and, naturally, there had been a big celebration afterward. Bill had ended up bringing Steve home an hour late and drunk . . . on a Sunday night, no less. The Chicago Catholic Leagues always played football on Sundays and Steve's dad, Ralph, was a strict man. Worse yet, he was religious and strict. So when Bill had brought Steve home late that night, he'd known he was headed for trouble.

Bill looked again at his watch. Steve was fifteen minutes late. *What's going on?* he thought to himself. Still, he waited in the open car. He was beginning to feel very chilly.

His mind drifted back to that night on the front porch. As Bill had walked Steve up the stairs to the front entrance, her father had burst through the door, yelling. Ralph had pulled his daughter inside and stepped back through the door to address Bill, who was, naturally, caught off guard. Mr. Stephen then grabbed Bill by both his collar and belt and physically lifted him off the front porch and threw him into the front yard. This was the first time Bill had ever *officially* flown.

When word of the incident spread, Bill's friends chose to make the best of it by teasing him remorselessly. For the better part of the year, the stories surrounding that night solidified Bill's reputation as a "wild man." Embarrassed as he was, Bill got some positive mileage out of it.

At last Steve came out of the house. She walked slowly and didn't wave. *Uh oh,* Bill thought. Steve got into the car and looked at Bill.

"Bill, why is the top down on this car?" She continued, "It may be sunny, but it's only thirty-six degrees out."

In his haste and fatigue, he hadn't realized that the top was still down. Even more curious, he couldn't remember when he had put it down. It must have been sometime between midnight and 5:00 a.m. Steve wasn't amused, and Bill knew it. He was in hot water.

"Bill," she started, looking straight ahead, "what time did you get in this morning? About 4:00 a.m.? Or was it five?" she continued.

She didn't *actually* want an answer, and Bill knew it. "Things have got to change, Bill."

Bill nodded. "Almost there. Oh damn, another red light!" He didn't realize he'd said that one out loud.

"Excuse me!" Steve shot back. She was enjoying seeing him squirm. In truth, she was a bit angry. It seemed as if Bill's wild streak was taking him over. His behavior was changing.

Bill put the car in park and raised the ragtop. As he did so, he again tried to remember when he had put the top down. All that came to mind was a dark night, Lake Shore Drive, and city lights. Since his morning hadn't started off very well, he figured he would keep those thoughts to himself.

As he got back in the car and began to drive again, Bill realized Steve wasn't sitting right beside him, as she usually did.

"Bill, this all night stuff is really getting to me," Steve stated sternly. Bill looked at her but said nothing. He knew she was right.

"Tell me, Bill," she continued "when you're out at night, do you go by Bill Cullerton or Johnny Lorenz? Hmm?"

Bill used John Lorenz as his professional football name. He did this so that if he went to college to play ball he would still be eligible, because once you played professional football, you would lose all college football eligibility.

"Steve, why would I do that? It never even occurred to me. Although I have to admit it is a pretty good idea."

Steve glared at him. Bill wasn't helping the cause. He had to act fast. "Steve, I don't know what to say. You know you're the only girl for me," he told her.

She rolled her eyes.

"Steve, I'm sorry. Can we go downtown for dinner tonight and cruise Lake Shore Drive? We'll go from north to south and back again, what do you think?" She looked at him and he smiled. She was starting to crack and he knew it.

Steve love-punched him on the shoulder. "You jerk!"

He puller her over to the middle of the seat and put his arm around her. "That's more like it," he said. "Steve, I hope you're coming to the big game on Sunday."

She looked at him and said, "I'll be there. What time does it start?"

"I've got a schedule in my book there on the floor."

She reached for the book and pulled the schedule out.

"Let's see. Sunday, December seventh, at . . . noon, Weber Stadium."

"Great, I'm glad you'll be there."

They arrived at Rosary College with little time to spare for Steve.

"I'll get a ride home this afternoon, Bill."

"I'll be by at seven, if that's okay."

"Perfect."

A quick kiss and Steve was off. Bill headed over to Wright College.

Weber Stadium, Chicago

December 7, 1941

It was a chilly Sunday at Chicago's Weber Stadium as the Austin Bears and the Berwyn Barons pounded each other up and down the field for the CFL Championship. There was a good crowd on hand, perhaps three or four thousand people. The CFL was a very popular semipro league in and around Chicago. There were several teams from Chicago and the near suburbs, but also those from as far away as suburban Elmhurst. Cigar smoke and air horns set the stage; the stands were nearly at capacity. It was exceptional football weather.

It was third down and three yards to go for Austin, late in the game. A running play was called to the right side in the huddle. On the previous play, in a pileup, Bill had taken punches to his ribs and face. These were the days before face masks. He was ticked off and ready to nail someone on the next play. The play was called. Bill, at the end position, would have to block a defensive tackle about forty pounds heavier than he was. It was an angle block, but he wasn't concerned.

As the play was called in the huddle, the broadcaster broke in on the public address system: "Attention please." He hesitated for a few seconds. "We have just received word that the Japanese have attacked Hawaii. It is reported that Pearl Harbor is under attack."

With further hesitation, he spoke, "Hawaii is preparing for a Japanese invasion. To repeat, Japan has attacked Pearl Harbor."

The players looked at each other and uttered some pretty stiff language. Bill looked toward the stands. With that grave announcement, they all knew what was coming. Steve and her friends were huddled under blankets in the stands. Steve looked down, rested her head on her left hand and closed her eyes. She knew that nothing in either her or Bill's life would ever be the same. Everyone stared into the distance. The time had come; America was in the war. Steve wondered if she and Bill would ever have a life together.

After an interval, the teams decided to cancel the remaining minutes of the game. It was too hard to concentrate, and everyone just wanted to go home.

Bill knew that if he had to go to war, his dream was to be a fighter pilot. They were the hotshots of the military. That was what he *really* wanted to be. So, after New Years Day, in 1942, he went down to the main recruiting station in Chicago to sign up for flight school in the Army Air Corps.

Aviation Cadet

In January of 1942, Bill signed up to be a US Army Air Corps cadet at the recruiting station in downtown Chicago. As soon as he signed his enlistment papers, the "authorities" grabbed Bill and took him over to Mayor Edward J. Kelly's office to take pictures for the newspapers. As the ten thousandth enlistee, he was to receive an all-expense-paid night out on the town, as well as spending a day as the Boy Mayor of Chicago. He met the real mayor, sat at his desk, and all of the newspapers in town took his picture for the evening news. Bill became a local celebrity overnight.

Then in the usual "hurry up and wait" military way, Bill and all the other cadet enlistees were told to go home and wait for the Army to call.

Later in 1942, by the time Cullerton was called to active duty after his reserve time, he had completed one year of college. He reported to Fort Sheridan in Wilmette, Illinois, to begin his year and a half of training.

That summer, Bill was assigned to sort parcel post in the back of an extremely large facility at the downtown Chicago post office. The new recruits assigned there took the army bus to and from work each day. The downtown post office was a monster of a building. After a week, Bill had gotten his routine down pretty well. He started to enjoy his time there, not to mention that three days a week Steve would meet him for lunch on the south rail dock underneath the building, in the open air.

Bill and Steve made the most of their summer lunchtimes at the post office. On their last lunch together before Bill left for Detroit, his buddies covered for him while he and Steve took a cab down to the lakefront, across Lake Shore Drive from Buckingham Fountain in Grant Park. They walked the lakefront hand in hand, talked about the future, and didn't waste a minute of their time together before he left for his next assignment.

To Detroit

1942

As an aviation cadet and officer in training in Detroit, Bill carried great responsibility. His job was at the main Detroit army enlistment center, where he sized the new recruits for their uniforms. He measured chest size, arm length, neck, height, and weight of new enlistees and draftees into the Army. It wasn't very exciting work but maybe better than sorting mail.

Cullerton had measured and weighed so many guys that he knew by the time they stepped up to his station exactly what their measurements would be. He had developed his visual measuring skills for his own good. The hygiene of these conscripts was terrible at best, and when he had to wrap a measuring tape under someone's supremely ripe armpit to get a chest measurement, well, it could be pretty rough. Without touching a measuring tape or scale, Cullerton would call out the sizes and weight of each guy down the line to his buddy, Harry Spencer, who was in charge of passing out the clothing.

One late fall day, while Cullerton was on duty at the Detroit recruitment center, Lieutenant Andrew Stone happened to be walking by his station. Stone, a fresh West Pointer, had quite a sadistic edge to him. He was a stiff who acted like a general and treated the cadets like West Point plebes. Today, he stopped beyond Cullerton's line of sight and watched him yell out the measurements to Harry, who had been trying to hint to Bill to stop: "Psssssssssst! Cully. Cully!"

"Cul-l-l-l-l-l-e-e-r-r-ton-n-n-n!"

Other cadets at nearby stations saw what was going on and kept watching from their posts. Spencer put his finger over his mouth in a "keep quiet" signal.

Cullerton continued. "Spencer, I'm busy right now. Can't you see I'm workin' here?" In his best interpretation of a carnival barker, Cullerton yelled out to Spencer, "Go away kid, yer botherin' me. Go get yer big sista and bring her back here. Can't you see I'm workin'? Hey, is she cute or does she look like you?"

The surrounding cadets couldn't hold back their laughter. They all looked away and covered their mouths, trying to keep their laughter quiet, but it was obvious and intense. They glanced at Cullerton and then over to Lieutenant Stone. Cullerton though his act was a hoot, so he kept it up. The next recruit in line was a six foot four, black recruit. Cullerton sat at his station, hands in pockets, and began shouting,

"All right, all right, step right up. Get your measurements here. There ya go big fella. Where ya from, sonny?

"From Hamtramck, Michigan, sir."

"Ham what, son?"

"Hamtramck."

"Sorry kid, didn't know if you could talk good." The cadets roared. The recruit was confused.

"Okay, Ham and Bacon, Michigan. Step right up. Okay, sonny, you're about six three. No, six four. Hey, Spence, put this kid down as a light-bulb inspector." Cullerton winked at the recruit, "We'll take care of ya, kid."

The laughter continued all around.

"What?" asked the recruit, "A light-bulb inspector?"

"Let's see, let's see. Okay, you're about two hundred and ten pounds. No, two hundred and fifteen. Big breakfast today, fella? Yep, two fifteen, Spence. Need to use the bathroom, sonny?"

Harry jotted the numbers down, chuckling all the while.

"Hey, man, how'd you know that?" questioned the recruit.

"There's plenty more where that came from, kid. Move along, let's get your arms and chest."

Lieutenant Stone watched in amazement, hands on his hips.

"Okay, sonny, stretch out your arms. Spence, we've got a twenty inch bicep here, seventeen inch neck, thirty-six inch sleeve and a forty-eight inch chest. Repeat, Spence, a forty-eight-inch chest. Hey, kid, you've got a big chest. Do you have a sister?"

The cadets were howling in the background.

"Get yer sista here and I'll give ya a shiny new dime." Even the recruit was smiling now.

The place erupted in laughter.

"Okay, sonny, step along and get your cotton candy. Move along, move along. Spence, give this kid a decoder ring. He's a good kid. Next, next. Step right up . . ."

Cullerton was on a roll. Spencer had written it all down, and by that time, Lieutenant Stone had seen enough.

"Cadet Cullerton."

"Sir."

"What do you think you are doing?"

He had caught Cullerton by surprise. Lieutenant Stone looked around and glared at the laughing cadets recruits. The guys stifled their laughter but anticipated more to come.

"Sir?" responded Cullerton, darting Harry an angry sideways glance.

"How can you measure a recruit without a tape measure or a scale, Cadet?"

"Sir, I have a gift, sir."

The cadets and recruits let out another laugh.

"Explain yourself, Cadet."

"Well, sir, I've seen enough recruits by now to know that I just know."

"Is that so, Cadet?"

"Yes, sir."

"Well, I find that hard to believe, Cadet."

Stone called the recruit back to Cullerton's station.

"Cadet Cullerton, remeasure this man, this time using Army regulation measuring tapes, scales, and height machines. If your measurements turn out to be different than what you yelled out to Cadet Spencer over there, then I'll have you inspecting genitals at the front of the line."

"Excuse me, sir, did you say I'll be inspecting generals?"

The laughter broke out again.

"No, Cadet, I said *genitals*. You'll be on crab patrol for the duration."

"For the duration of the shift, sir?"

"For the duration of the war, Cadet." Laughter erupted again; Lieutenant Stone had scored.

"Sir, judging by these fine recruits, that's a lot of crabs, sir."

"Yes it is, Cadet. But you'll also be a crab expert." The cadets and recruits applauded the lieutenant's. second score.

As Cullerton began to remeasure the recruit, the laughter simmered; the guys were placing bets now. As the recruit got on the scale, Lieutenant Stone yelled out the limits.

"Cadet Cullerton, I will give you three, no, two and a half pounds in either direction of weight, and three fourths of an inch either direction. As for the neck, only one half inch, either way. Okay, Cadet, let's get the weight out of the way."

The recruit stepped on the scale and it leveled off at two hundred twelve and a half pounds. Cullerton exhaled in relief; the crowd cheered. Lieutenant Stone broke in, "Cullerton, is your family in the circus; are they circus folk?"

Everyone laughed again.

"Are you a gypsy, son? Are you some kind of a circus clown? Do you wear clown makeup? Do you work in a circus or have relatives in the circus? Do you aspire to be a carnival professional? Is your mother the bearded lady? Are you a ringer, son?"

Even Bill began laughing at the attention and replied in the negative to each question. So the measuring continued. Cullerton was within all tolerances of the measuring until the final measurement of the recruit's neck. Cullerton measured.

"Seventeen and one half inches."

There was a dead silence in the room before the chaos began. Money changed hands. The lieutenant pursed his lips in mock frustration, but there was a smiling glint in his eyes. Stone looked around. *This is good*, he thought. *This is building morale and camaraderie.* Stone knew that many of the men in the room would soon be off to war and many of them would not make it back. He could live with their laughter and having fun, but only briefly. There was a war to attend to, after all.

"Lieutenant, sir," said Cullerton, approaching and saluting, "Lieutenant, shall I stay at my position?"

"Yes, Cadet, but occasionally use the measuring equipment. We wouldn't want one of these guys uncomfortable with tight-fitting underwear."

"Yes, sir; okay, sir." Cullerton saluted.

"By the way, Cadet, where did you get your routine?"

"At Riverview Amusement Park in Chicago, as a visitor, sir."

"Riverview? Is that like Coney Island Amusement Park in New York?"

"Well, sir, I've not been to New York, but I believe that is correct."

"Carry on, Cadet."

"Thank you, sir." They both saluted.

Cullerton's buddies patted him on the back as they got back to business. They all agreed that Lieutenant Stone wasn't such a bad guy after all.

After the war, Bill could outguess any carny doing body weights at a carnival.

To Flight School

One year after signing up for the Army Air Corps, Bill finally got his orders to report to Kelly Field in San Antonio, Texas, for classroom training. Bill was nervous; he knew that classroom training was going to be his biggest hurdle. He was an intelligent kid, but aeronautics was going to be difficult for him to grasp. Bill had worked as hard as he could when attending Wright College and knew that he only had one chance to become a fighter pilot. He and his buddy from Chicago, Harry Spencer, rode the train from Detroit to San Antonio, giving them plenty of time to discuss what lay ahead.

As Bill and his class of nearly one thousand cadets began their training, so began the weeding-out process. This was Air Corps ground school classroom training, including aeronautics, engineering, and other less-than-exciting coursework. Bill progressed, but at his first crucial review, a counselor told him that he was not scoring well enough to become a fighter pilot, let alone a "regular" pilot. Bill was not deterred; he promised to keep working hard and to improve. The counselor must have sensed something in him, or perhaps Bill was a genuine salesman, because they didn't bounce him out as they had intended to do at the meeting. Instead, they decided to keep him in the advanced classroom program. In the end, Bill just barely passed. He passed with the absolute minimum score of seventy percent. Sixty-nine percent was failing, and with that would come a one-way ticket to basic boot camp as an army grunt. Four hundred of the original one thousand cadets had been washed out at this point. The class was getting smaller. However, the year at Wright College had paid off; Bill was continuing on.

The next stop was the military aviation base at Stanford, Texas, for the Primary Flight Training course. The six hundred remaining cadets would finally get to fly; this course was not for the faint of heart. After only six hours of intense assisted flight, their training included stalls and spins initiated by onboard trainers. Would-be pilots were weeded out every day. After that short term of assisted flight time, the cadets had to fly solo in the Fairchild PT-19 airplane. The cadet dropout rate was expected and intended to be high at this point because of the imminent danger of flight in war. The Army Air Corps needed to move the most qualified cadets rapidly through the system and to reassign those that did not make the grade.

At Stanford, the cadets also learned to fly lazy eights, rolls, turns, and spins. They had to stall the plane in flight and recover alone. The cadets had to be familiar with all of these maneuvers in their trainer aircraft. There were fighter accidents, and some deaths occurred. By the end of Primary Flight Training, another thirty percent of the original class was gone, and the original air cadet class of one thousand was now down to three hundred members. By the second level of training, seventy percent of the air force cadets had washed out. Meanwhile, Bill seemed to be in his element whenever he was in an airplane, and he was moving to the top of the list for candidacy as a fighter pilot.

After Primary Flight Training, the three hundred "survivors" of Bill's group moved on to Winfield, Kansas, for Basic Flying Training. Here, the training was far more intense, challenging, and dangerous. Bill and Harry Spencer would make the trip and the cut together.

Basic Flying Training was a "basic plus" flight training school. The cadets learned aerial coordination and flying maneuvers of all types, included attacking, diving, and evasion. The flight requirements were getting tougher, and Bill was getting better. He was a natural in fighter-sized aircraft; he was an aggressive pilot, and it did not go unnoticed by his fellow cadets and instructors. Others, however, did not fare as well.

At this point of the training, some cadets would not become pilots, as their flying skills were not improving. Rather, they might show an aptitude for navigation and be reassigned to become navigators on the bombers. Some had skills better suited to accurately bombing targets; they would be reassigned to bombardier training. Other cadets were likely to be excellent pilots, but pilots of a more cautious nature. Make no mistake; the Army wanted these capable, cautious pilots. Caution was a skill required for the highly regarded bomber pilots and copilots, as well as transport plane and rescue pilots.

The navigation, bombardier, and pilot cadet candidates were all moved to Bomber Command and continued their training there. Fighter pilots needed to be of a less cautious and more aggressive nature, with catlike reactions while flying at three hundred fifty miles per hour. Fighter pilots had to have excellent maneuvering skills at the highest of speeds and have an "edge," an intangible asset that would make a fighter pilot stand out. As Bill once put it, "The army wanted guys that were a little stupid to be fighter pilots." With Bill's aggressive nature, it was not surprising that he passed his psychological test for fighter pilots with flying colors.

After Winfield, the fifty remaining cadets (of the original one thousand) who had not been washed out or reassigned to bombers were transferred to Foster Field at Victoria, Texas, for the last level of fighter pilot training. This was Advanced Pilot Training, where cadets' skills had to continue to progress, or they would be transferred out. Some of the cadets who made it to Foster Field would be reassigned to become bomber pilots, but most made it through to become fighter pilots.

Cadet Cullerton would have to pass this course to get his wings. Once he received his fighter pilot wings, he would be commissioned as a Second Lieutenant in the United States Army Air Corps. At Foster Field he again impressed his instructors, and he completed the advanced class at the end of 1943, with the graduation ceremony in January of 1944. The first class to graduate that year at Victoria Field was a mere thirty of the original one thousand cadets. Bill and Harry Spencer both received their wings. The reality was that only three percent of those cadets who wished to become fighter pilots would realize their dream. Bill and his buddies had earned the right to be a little bit cocky.

Second Lieutenant

Foster Field, Victoria, Texas
Graduation Day
January 1944

Bill Cullerton stepped forward when his name was called. He saluted the colonel and received his wings.

"Second Lieutenant William J. Cullerton, wear these silver wings proudly on your lapel. Congratulations, Lieutenant, you are now a United States Army Air Corps officer, gentleman, and fighter pilot." Bill stated later on that receiving his wings as a fighter pilot was his proudest moment in the military.

With these words, Second Lieutenant William J. Cullerton of Chicago, Illinois, and the other twenty-nine members of class 44A at Foster Field, Texas, were graduated from advanced US Army Air Corps fighter training school. After all they had gone through during the last thirteen months, the new officers headed off to one more training center for their final class. The class was located at Hillsborough Air Base near Tampa, Florida, at the higher level of Advanced Fighter Training School. At Hillsborough, the new second lieutenants would train on the advanced versions of the P-51 Mustang fighter aircraft, the aircraft they would be flying in combat. The new pilots would be taught by veteran fighter pilots who had flown in Europe and the Mediterranean. The new pilots from class 44A had one more rung of the ladder to climb, and then it would be their turn to go to war.

There was one very important skill that Cullerton and his classmates would learn at Hillsborough. They were going to be trained to strafe; strafing was an art as well as a skill. The pilots were trained to fly as low as twenty-five feet above the ground, at speeds of two hundred fifty and three hundred fifty miles per hour. They were trained to not fear the ground level attack. They learned low level skip bombing; they learned how to strafe a train by shooting apart the tracks underneath the locomotive; and they learned how to attack a German airfield, including the correct speed, altitudes, and gun angles for the best results. At Hillsborough they trained for the low level attack, and by the time the pilots completed advanced training at Hillsborough, Cullerton's group was a bit more comfortable with it than earlier pilots, who had learned these skills, at a high cost, in actual combat. The new pilots got comfortable flying fifty feet above the ground. Most pilots preferred the air-to-air action at twenty thousand feet, but Cullerton loved the ground level attack.

Even more importantly, Bill's class was the first class to train in the newest and most improved version of the North American Aviation made P51 Mustang. The plane was outfitted with the bubbletop canopy, improved wings and improved powerplant. The Mustang had the Merlin Engine, built by Packard, in the US, under license from Rolls Royce Motors of Britain. The P-51D, when modified in the field, could fly at nearly 500 mph and remained extremely agile. It was deadly in the thin air at 25,000 feet, with its famous supercharger. It was armed with six .50 caliber machine guns, three in each wing. Two 75 gallon fuel tanks, mounted underneath the wing, gave the P-51D a range in excess of 1600 miles. This was great for escorting bombers to and from Germany, but also excellent for the vast distances of the Pacific theater. The cost of each Mustang in 1944 was about $50,000.

In early 1944, when General Doolittle took command of the US Eighth Air Force (AF) in Europe, he expanded on the order that pilots strafe all German military targets. His scorched earth strategy was to destroy Germany's ability to effectively wage war by destroying their airplanes, locomotives, and other vehicles in greater numbers than the Germans could replace them. In effect, it would be a war of attrition.

Fighter pilots like numbers. The higher the kill numbers the better. So pilots began to descend into the dangerous low altitudes to attack German aerodromes and airfields. Strafing scores began to pile up in the Eighth AF. The Eighth was losing more pilots to German ground fire, but the Germans were beginning to lose aircraft, tanks, and trains faster than they could replace them. Doolittle's strategy was working.

General Doolittle felt that an airplane destroyed on the ground was as important as an airplane destroyed in the sky.

Everyone knew that the Germans were extremely effective in shooting down low-flying Allied aircraft. In fact, more Allied fighter planes were lost to ground fire than aerial combat in the war. The result was that most American pilots were reluctant to strafe. Fighter Command was aware of this reluctance in its pilots, so General Doolittle upped the ante. The order went out that each plane destroyed on the ground counted equally to an aerial victory. Only in the Eight Air Force did a strafing kill equal an aerial kill.

Bill Cullerton's "action" football photo in his senior year at
Fenwick High in Oak Park.

Cullerton and two ground crewmembers in a popular photo.
Note Cullerton's headgear on one of the two rearview mirrors that
were on the P-51D models. 1944.

First Lieutenant Bill Cullerton at home in Chicago, Christmas of 1944, for a war bond tour, between his first and second flight tours. Bill had 4 aerial and 14 ground kills at this point. The war bond tour would be cut short due to the Battle of the Bulge.

Built around 1100, this Normal style cathedral, known as St. Catherine's.
Provided a landmark for returning pilots with its four-storey tower.
St. Catherine's is in Litlington, near the Steeple Morden air base.

Another shot of Bill on the wing of the "Miss Steve." Note the 10 Nazi
markers on the base of his canopy. The plane has been prepped for long
a distance mission with the under-wing fuel tanks.

Although Cullerton looks very young here at the age of 21

. . . the German airfield gunners were in their midteens.

Logo of the 355th FG at the Steeple Morden Memorial
Motto: "Our Might Always"

Off to War

Cullerton, Spencer, and many others stood at the rails of the foredeck of the *Queen Mary* as it steamed out of the Port of New Jersey. Everyone wanted to see the Statue of Liberty. Lady Liberty stood as a clear reminder of what this whole war was about. The great ocean liner maneuvered out of the Hudson River and toward open water. There was quiet on the deck as they all watched the New York skyline and the shoreline of the United States fade in the distance before finally disappearing beyond the horizon. At this point, everyone turned and began to look forward, toward Europe, and many of the men began to wonder if this might be a one-way trip.

The *Queen Mary* was steaming at full speed; Bill would arrive in Scotland in just sixty-four hours. America already seemed far away, and home was only a dream. The new officers enjoyed all of the amenities the ship had to offer. But rather than spending all of their time in the Officer's Club, many of the men preferred to gaze over the handrails of the ship, allegedly for the uninterrupted ocean panorama, but many of them were really watching for telltale signs of torpedoes. They were familiar with the story of the *Lusitania*, the famous British luxury ship during World War I, which was sunk by a German submarine while on its way home from American. Thus, the soldiers were edgy, and some were a little seasick, but all in all this was a much better ride than in a steel-gray Yankee troop transport.

The great ship traveled alone on her voyage, and the only reason she traveled alone was that no other ship could keep up with her. The *Queen Mary* traveled at thirty knots per hour (thirty-five miles per hour) all the way across the Atlantic, in an effort to outrun everything, particularly the German U-boats. They crossed the Atlantic in only three days, and harbored in the Port of Edinburgh, Scotland.

Once the *Queen Mary* docked, Bill and some of his new pilot buddies began the long train ride down to London and out to Cambridge. It was early in June 1944, and there was activity everywhere. As the train traveled south, Bill admired the pastoral scenery, the stone houses, and the wet, green, misty hills. He watched the farming activities and it reminded him of old-time farming in the upper peninsula of Michigan. Horses or mules pulled wagons and plows; laborers worked by hand in the fields. He saw century-old buildings, still in use. The more he looked the more beautiful and surreal the environment became. It was so different from the west side of Chicago.

The ride was comfortable, and the Scots and Brits were all friendly to the Yanks, which helped the young soldiers become acquainted with their new home for the duration of the war.

Bill and the other new pilots had arrived in Britain on the eve of the invasion of the European continent. Operation Overload, known later as D-Day, was only forty-eight hours away, unbeknownst to the pilots. They had arrived on the eve of the greatest military invasion in history. Bill and Spencer were going to fly what would become known as the greatest fighter airplane ever built.

Steeple Morden

June 4, 1944, Lieutenant Cullerton and his fellow rookie pilots arrived in Cambridge, England. The pilots had some time before catching a bus to Steeple Morden, which was several miles outside of Cambridge, an incredibly beautiful city. Cullerton and his buddies were awestruck by the Gothic beauty and age of the city. No place in America looked like or felt anything like Cambridge, England. It was a medieval city, older than the United States. It centered on a river and was home to nearly thirty of the greatest institutions of higher education in the world, the universities at Cambridge. The universities dominated the city, and its magnificent buildings were inspirational. The Yanks walked the narrow streets and felt the presence of history and traditions in this amazing English city. Although awestruck by their new surroundings, the soldiers began to feel very far away from home. The people there were friendly, but not overly friendly. But after a brief walk around the great university, and stopping in a couple of pubs, of course, the Americans began to feel a bit better about things, and they caught the next bus to the remote village of Steeple Morden.

On the way to Steeple Morden, Cullerton and Spencer hooked up with fellow pilots: Bert Marshall Jr., Royce Priest, Charles Hauver, Jack Crandell, and Fred Haviland. On narrow rural streets, their bus drove on the "wrong" side of the road. The English countryside was beautiful and lushly green in the damp June weather. Rolling hills showed signs of some of the early crops beginning to sprout. Tree lines and stone walls separated the farms; old stone and stucco buildings were the standard farmhouses. There were some tractors at the farms, but often the fields were being plowed by horses and women were planting the seeds. In both England and America the men had gone to war and women were filling the labor pool, more so in England, for it had been at war longer and was paying a very high price in human life.

The bus drove into the small town of Litlington, adjacent to Steeple Morden. Like Steeple Morden, Litlington was a small farm town with only a few hundred residents during peacetime. The famous St. Catherine's Church, built in the years around 1100 AD, was a landmark for the pilots who flew in and out of the Steeple Morden airbase. St. Catherine's had been nearly four hundred years old when Columbus bumped into the Western Hemisphere. The bus continued on through to the next town, Steeple Morden. This was the town where the United States Eighth Air Force's 355th Fighter Group was based. The American fighter group took over the air base in 1943, after the Royal Air Force (RAF) relocated its air group that had been based there to another rural location in England.

The bus continued on Litlington Road, passing through the town before heading out to the American base. Some people who were outside waved to the Americans and the new guys waved back. The Americans saw a school, administration building, church, and many picturesque houses. The houses in Steeple Morden were brick, and many had authentic thatched roofs; they were classic rural England homes. They were close together, and the main road wove neatly through the fairytale town.

To the new replacement pilots on their way to the air base; Steeple Morden looked to be a town where, in peaceful times, one would have the feeling it hadn't changed much in two hundred years.

It was a beautiful city to the Americans, and they began to love it immediately. They knew they were in England and were guests of the English. The English residents had embraced American visitors when the base opened in 1943 and often invited the Americans into their homes for dinner and conversation. The young kids of Steeple Morden and Litlington would go over to the air base and talk with the Americans, who would treat the youngsters very well. The children would go to the edges of the runways and lie in the grass, watching the Mustangs land and take off right over their heads. Lifelong relationships were bound to develop between the wonderful British citizens of Litlington and Steeple Morden and the Americans who were based there.

The bus finally arrived at the airbase. The new men saw the American flag and felt more relaxed at the sight of their own Stars and Stripes. The expedition was over. As Cullerton stepped off the bus, he recapped the journey in his mind, back to when he had dined at Hackney's Steakhouse in New Jersey. It seemed like years ago, yet it had only been about eight days since he had said goodbye to the United States.

The bus pulled away from the base, while ten new replacement pilots stood in the dirt, watching the activity of the American air base. It was about 3:00 p.m. in Steeple Morden, and overhead, fighters were returning from a mission. As the new pilots watched, their pulses raced with anticipation. This was it. A sergeant approached them, saluted, and offered to escort the officers to meet the commanding officer before guiding them to their quarters.

The new guys got the quick tour of the base. They were told to become familiar with their surroundings until their planes were ready. The new pilots were anxious, swinging between excitement and nervousness for what was to come. They were eager to fly, which was part of the Army's plan.

Cullerton was assigned to the 357th Fighter Squadron (FS). The 355th Fighter Group (FG) was comprised of three fighter squadrons: the 354th, the 357th, and the 358th. All three of these fighter groups had mascots. The 354th FG had the English Bulldog named "Yank" as their mascot. The 357th FG had the fire breathing dragon. The 358th FG had the protective Angel.

The 355th Fighter Group was one of seventeen fighter groups in the Eighth Air Force who were stationed in England and fighting in Europe. All of the fighter groups were competitive with each other, as each wanted to be the best fighter group in the Eighth Air Force. By the end of the war, it was arguable that the 355th Fighter Group might have been General Doolittle's favorite. As it turned out, the pilots of the 355th Fighter Group were to become, statistically, the greatest strafing fighter group of the war, and Bill Cullerton was destined to become one of the greatest strafers in the entire US Eighth Air Force.

After meeting everyone in charge and being debriefed on the upcoming assignments, the new group was taken to their quarters. The truck dropped off Captain Marshall, and Lieutenants Priest and Hauver at the field office of the 354th FS. All seven pilots shook hands. "See you tomorrow at 0400, boys," one of the lieutenants called out.

"Yeah, we'll see you guys there," replied one of the new pilots. The truck moved on to drop off Cullerton, Crandell, Haviland, and Spencer at the field office of the 357th FS.

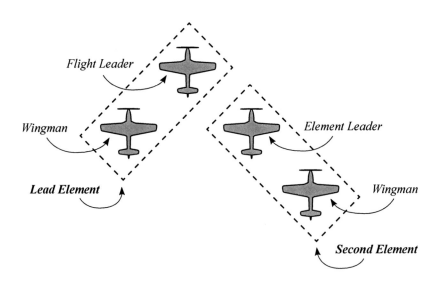

One "Flight" has four aircraft paired into two Elements as shown above. The Flight Leader is also an Element Leader. All new pilots started out as Wingmen and moved along with accruing flight experience, and skill, eventually to become Element Leaders and perhaps Flight Leaders.

4 Flights equal a Squadron of 16 aircraft.
3 Squadrons complete a Flight Group.
  (See Figure 2)

Figure 1: A FLIGHT FORMATION

Replacement Pilots

Steeple Morden
June 4, 1944

Well, that's what they were . . . replacements. Cullerton and the other new guys were here to replace other pilots, but that wasn't as ominous as it sounded. Not every replacement pilot was for a downed flier. Rather, most veteran pilots who had finished their tour of duty were rotated back to the States or went home on leave. Occasionally pilots were invited to fly a second three-hundred hour tour. These pilots were distinguished flyers and had the option to decline the offer and instead rotate back to the States and become an instructor or hold an administrative position; however, many would accept the offer and take the second tour. Flying a second tour meant pushing your luck, especially as a strafing pilot.

Flying actual combat missions, such as bomber escort missions, patrol missions, or even Mustang bombing missions, requires tremendous organization, strategy, precision, and discipline. American fighter pilots fly in a *flight*, in a V-formation made up of four aircraft (two pair). The first pair, called the *lead element*, consists of the flight leader (very front) and his wingman. The second pair, called the *second element*, consists of an element leader and *his* wingman. Four of these flights make up a squadron (sixteen aircraft), and finally, three squadrons make up an entire flight group (forty-eight aircraft).

In a flight, where the lead element goes, the others follow. The second element has some discretionary authority, and the wingmen are there to protect their leader. For this reason, wingmen aren't able to fly off and engage the enemy on their own; only the leaders can. The wingmen can advance position within the flight by mastering and proving their skills to eventually become leaders.

A new pilot had to pay his dues, based upon how he handled his opportunities and how well he learned his job as a wingman. An exceptional wingman would be able to perform his job in total accuracy, protect his leader, and at the same time observe real combat tactics and flight maneuvers. Observation of these would allow the wingman to see how both sides engaged, resulting in better flight and fight technique. It was important for the new fliers to learn more on each mission, as the chance to engage the enemy in flight would happen sooner or later. Therefore, every pilot had to be prepared or else his number would be up very quickly.

It was June 4, 1944, the day that Cullerton had been waiting for since that Sunday afternoon on the football field in December of 1941. It had been a long road and now, after two and a half years, Cullerton was going to fly his first combat mission as an American fighter pilot, flying the most advanced fighter aircraft in the world. While he followed the pilots from the ready room to the planes, Bill's stomach tossed and turned, though he managed to appear outwardly calm. He had been assigned as a wingman to Captain Les Minshew, the element leader. *Good God. A captain,* Cullerton thought. Captain Minshew approached the new second lieutenant and said, "Whatever you do, do not leave my side." Minshew continued to walk toward his plane while Cullerton stood there attempting to salute.

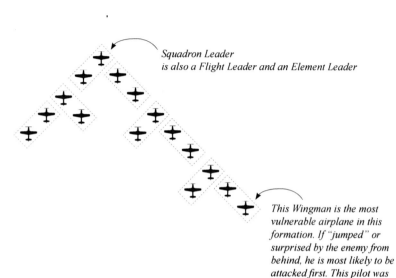

*Squadron Leader
is also a Flight Leader and an Element Leader*

*This Wingman is the most
vulnerable airplane in this
formation. If "jumped" or
surprised by the enemy from
behind, he is most likely to be
attacked first. This pilot was
often nicknamed "Purple Heart
Charlie" or "Tail End Charlie"
in a gallows humor context by
the other pilots. Often times,
an experienced pilot would
take this position.*

*This is a Squadron (16 aircraft).
There are 3 squadrons in a complete Flight Group
or, in this case Fighter Group.*

The 355th Fighter Group (FG) was based at Steeple Morden near Cambridge in Southeast England. The 355th FG was comprised principally of three Squadrons. These Squadrons were the 354th Fighter Squadron (FS) known as the "Bulldogs", the 357th FS known as the "Dragons", and the 358th FS known as the "Angels". Additionally, there were executive and administrative level senior pilots who were assigned to an "HQ" designated Fighter Group, and the 355th FG also included the 2nd Scout Force. This group flew well ahead of the bombers to advise of weather patterns and to look for the Luftwaffe.

Figure 2: A SQUADRON FORMATION

Cullerton, replied, "Yes, sir," but Minshew chose not to hear it, and he kept on. Cullerton hesitated for a moment, brought down his salute, and ran over to his plane, which the ground crew had readied.

Minshew was an experienced pilot with several aerial victories already and was a good guy overall. He had first flown the beloved P-47 Thunderbolts, known affectionately as Jugs (short for water jugs), at Steeple Morden. The entire base had recently been switched to the longer range, more agile, but more fragile Mustangs. At twenty-six years old, Minshew was much older than twenty-one year old Cullerton.

On June 4, 1944, the mission of the 355th FG was to patrol an area in France from Abbeville to Amien to Cambria, and then over to St. Valaray, before returning home. Although the patrol did not encounter any German resistance, one of the fighters was hit by flak, which caused his plane to crash on the beach. It was Cullerton's first combat flight, and he had already witnessed one plane crash and the death of a pilot. Cullerton was shaken up by the unexpected casualty and began to fear for his life, wondering if he would be next.

"Welcome to air combat!" Minshew announced over the intercom. Cullerton, still shaken up, brushed off his nerves and then vowed to never worry like that again. *If your time is up, then so be it,* he thought to himself. This fatalistic attitude was one of the realities that all flight crews in war had to adopt. Still, this was Cullerton's first mission, and he was nervous as hell. He never took his eyes off Minshew's plane; he held a strong wingman position. After landing, Cullerton couldn't remember where he had been or anything he had seen, with the exception of Captain Minshew's plane and, of course, the Mustang that had gone down.

Cullerton flew another mission on June 5. It was a short bombing mission across the English Channel. All planes were back early and prepped for the next day. The pilots watched as the ground crews painted black and white "invasion" stripes around each wing and on both sides of the fuselages of every aircraft.

A base meeting was called for midnight, June 6, when Cullerton and the other new guys sat in the rear of the hall and listened. Once it was confirmed that this was *the* invasion, Cullerton's mind drifted back, as he thought of everything he had done since he joined the Army in early 1942, including sorting mail at the main Chicago Post Office. Now here he was, a rookie pilot about to fly a mission, his third mission, on what the brass were now calling D-Day.

Bill wondered what the odds were of him joining the Army as a pilot cadet back in 1942 and ending up here at Steeple Morden, in his own airplane, on the eve of the invasion of Europe, at the very beginning of his flying career for Uncle Sam. Bill knew that he was in the right place at the right time with the right aircraft. Knowing this, he silently promised to do everything he could and to do it well.

The commanding officer of the 355th FG, Colonel Cummings, told the men that in order to support the Allied invasion at Normandy, each of the three fighter squadrons would fly three missions a day for several days in support of the landings. Normally, the primary effort of the 355th FG was to provide fighter cover for the bombers both to and from their designated sites. To support the invasion, they were to bomb, strafe, and disrupt all German military efforts to reinforce and increase German resistance at the beaches in Normandy. Colonel Cummings cautioned the pilots not to shoot civilian rail or road traffic. This baffled many of the pilots; they scratched their heads and exchanged glances of confusion. The flight routes of the various missions had been planned to avoid the shipping lanes during Allied beach landings to help avoid friendly fire casualties.

D-Day

June 6, 1944

Cullerton flew in the second mission flown by the 357th FG on D-Day. This was a fighter bomber mission. Each plane carried two 250-pound bombs. The fighter group commanding officer, Colonel Cummings, led their group over to France, as they pounded bridges, tanks, and supply columns that were headed to the coast. Cullerton's bombs hit a bridge and strafed a military convoy. They all made it back to Steeple Morden, save one, who was hit by flak.

For the next eleven days, in support of the invasion, pilots flew one, two, and sometimes three missions a day. This was valuable, intense training and indoctrination for the new pilots.

The pilots of the 357th FS reported that Lieutenant George Phillips was the pilot who had been hit by flak. He had bailed out, but when he bailed, he had hit the tail of his plane; his chute had never opened and he had fallen to his death.

Cullerton was walking over to the officer's club and thinking about Phillips. Phillips had been a new pilot, like himself. He hadn't known him well, but just like most of the guys, Phillips had been likable. Cullerton had been out several times now and two new pilots in his squadron had been killed, both as a result of flak. *Heck*, he thought, *Phillips survived the flak and was killed when he bailed.* It just didn't seem right. Cullerton was beginning to realize how dangerous his job really was, and he hadn't even seen any enemy aircraft yet. But he loved what he was doing anyway and was determined to make his mark.

At the officer's club, the men talked, and they heard that the invasion was going well. They went outside to watch the third mission head to France. When they went back inside, Cullerton saw Bert Marshall and congratulated him on his first aerial victory on only his second mission. Marshall was "buying" the drinks that night.

On June 20, Cullerton's squadron got into a serious aerial engagement with enemy fighters. Cullerton was Minshew's wingman again and stayed with him as Minshew attacked the leading Messerschmitt 109. They battled until Minshew destroyed the enemy plane. Cullerton did his job and learned all he could from the experience.

There was standard Army procedure upon returning from a mission. When the pilots landed, they were immediately picked up and taken to the debriefing room. They were all given a shot or two of brandy, as an icebreaker. It didn't take long for the pilots to start talking about the mission. Staff officers observed, asked questions, and took notes. This was crucial to the assessment of the day's activities for the success or failure of a particular mission. Although there was film in the gun cameras of each plane, the verbal information was crucial to assessing the mission in concert with the film.

Throughout June, Cullerton flew several missions. He was flying with the best, Colonel Clairborne Kinnard and Major Henry Kucheman. He flew as a wingman for both, as well as for Minshew, through most of July. He didn't get a chance for aerial combat; however, this summer allowed him time to hone his skills. His time would come; he was moving up quickly. Toward the end of July, he would be up to become an element leader, and with this promotion, his chances for engaging the enemy were getting better.

An Ace on the Deck

On August 16, 1944, the 357th FS was escorting a bomber group to Germany when more than twenty enemy fighters jumped them. It was a wild aerial engagement. Thirteen German aircraft were downed, four pilots of the 357th destroyed two enemy aircraft apiece, and five pilots destroyed an enemy fighter each, with a loss of only one pilot and his Mustang.

Lieutenant Bill Cullerton got his first two aerial victories.

The best opportunity for a fighter pilot to win an aerial engagement is simple: attack another fighter before he sees you. The element of surprise is yours if you can "bounce" or "jump" the fighters from behind, above, or from the direction of the sun, where the enemy can't see you. Both the Allies and the Germans used these tactics.

The fighters who fly bomber escort are usually above the bombers, looking for the enemy fighters. A cynical person might see this scenario as using the bombers for bait, when in reality, the escort fighters might have the element of surprise, and the bombers, after all, do have a mission to complete. Obviously, the bombers are slower and less maneuverable than the fighters, but the bombers carry incredible defensive firepower and can be deadly to enemy fighters, as well.

This day, the Germans changed strategy. The Germans spotted the American bombers and fighters first, and "bounced" the American fighters rather than attacking the bombers. The pilots of the 357th responded in an organized scramble to outmaneuver the attackers after the Germans attacked the far-left wing of the flight group formation. Cullerton, of Blue Flight, looked over his shoulder as someone yelled, "Messerschmitt, Messerschmitt!" (the first warning over the radio).

"One-oh-nine, on your tail, Blue Flight."

"Drop tanks."

With that order, sixty-three long range fuel tanks immediately dropped from the wings of the Mustangs.

"Break left, Blue Flight."

And the melee at twenty thousand feet began. More than twenty German Me 109s and FW 190s attacked the American fighter escort rather than the bombers. This was a bold move by the Germans, and at first it surprised the Americans.

Blue Flight broke left into tight circles to come around on the attacking Germans. He zeroed in on one of the last 109s. He called to his wingman, Lieutenant John Riggs: "Riggs, Riggs" There was no response.

When Cullerton looked over, his wingman was gone. He was alone, and there were three 109s after him. He went defensive immediately, pulling tight circles so the enemy fighters could not get any deflection shots on him. He called for assistance over the radio as he circled tighter. It would only be a few more moments until the third Messerschmitt trailing him would have the angle on him, as the first two enemy fighters forced him into the tight circles.

"Custard 97, calling for immediate assistance. I've got three of these bastards on me!"

"Repeat—Custard 97 needs assistance."

As Cullerton kept looking over both shoulders, Crandell dove down and shot up the leader of the three Jerries on Cullerton's tail. The other two planes broke, and Cullerton went after one. He shot a burst and missed. As the Jerry turned, Cullerton fired inside his turn, nearly six hundred feet away. The tail of the German fighter broke off, the plane went down, and Cullerton had his first aerial victory. He had no time to think about it; the engagement was still in progress. He spotted another Jerry below him and dove down. He was right behind him and got him with the first burst. The Jerry did a quick roll and dove upside down for the deck. With adrenaline coursing through his system, Bill chased the German down to about five hundred feet above the ground. The Jerry continued to roll his plane in an attempt to escape, but Cullerton fired another short burst and the German plane went down. He crash landed and skidded a long distance as Cullerton made another pass. The Jerry fighter came to rest against a tree. Cullerton had destroyed two German aircraft in the melee, and Jack Crandell had saved Bill's life.

This engagement lasted nearly a half an hour before the Germans broke off. Lieutenants Bill Cullerton and Harry Spencer, friends since basic training, had destroyed two enemy aircraft each and Crandell had destroyed one. As far as Cullerton was concerned, Crandell had gotten the most important one. All told, thirteen enemy aircraft were destroyed. The lone Mustang lost was that of Cullerton's wingman, Lieutenant John Riggs. Since Cullerton was the flight leader when the Jerries bounced, the Jerries had gone after him and, of course, his wingman. Cullerton, although very good, had gotten lucky that day. He intended to "buy" Crandell a drink at the officer's club that night and to propose a toast to Lieutenant Riggs.

It was later determined that one of Lieutenant Riggs's fuel tanks had not released. He had last been seen headed for the deck in a spin with two Germans on his tail. Since the Americans had been outnumbered in the attack, no one had been able to immediately join the chase for Riggs. At one point, two Mustangs had broken free and gone after Riggs, but they had not been able to find him.

Cullerton did not realize it, but back at Steeple Morden he was being watched. The press was always nearby during the war. Good news or bad, news was news, and it needed to be reported. Since Cullerton had gained local celebrity status in Chicago as the ten thousandth Army Air Corps Cadet signed up in Chicago (in a promotional effort by the *Chicago Times* newspaper and the Army), the newspaper quietly watched as Cullerton progressed through flight training. When he received his wings, the newspaper ran an article about it. Wisely enough, the *Times* did not overhype Cullerton's graduation as a pilot. Cullerton had claimed two aerial victories. *Now* there was a story to tell.

A Good Tip

The German V-1 "buzz" bomb began to gently arc downward toward London as it reached its zenith over the English Channel. The unmanned German rocket, which was the world's first cruise missile, would be able to bolt across the sky at almost three hundred miles an hour, streaming fire from its revolutionary rocket propulsion system. This particular bomb had excellent direction and trajectory. In only a few minutes, nearly fifty people would die as it struck its target. If this rocket were to hit a hospital, a government building, or a church, perhaps nearly five hundred civilians could be expected to die. One way or another, this missile was on a course to cause great damage in central London.

In the distance, and from an altitude of five thousand feet, the pilot of an American P-51 Mustang fighter aircraft saw the telltale rocket flame below and immediately knew what was happening. The Mustang accelerated rapidly and dove toward the exhaust flame. The chase was on, and there wasn't much time to lose. The Mustang had to get to the rocket quickly, before the rocket reached landfall. The Mustang was diving at nearly five hundred miles an hour as the supercharger engaged on the mystical Merlin engine. The Mustang began to close the gap on the German rocket. As the pilot focused on the flying bomb ahead, the G-forces were strong on the American pilot, causing three sweeping turns and a full roll.

The Mustang began to level off and rapidly approached the rocket from behind. The Mustang pilot slowed the plane down to match the rocket's speed, constantly adjusting the Mustang's angle of descent to match the German rocket's continuous change in elevation.

The pilot looked up and over to his right; the rocket was a mere twenty feet away from him. Slowly, and with great precision, the pilot brought the Mustang's right wing up and closer to the V-1's stubby left wing. The flame on this flying bomb was now only eighteen feet from the pilot's face. Together the two aircraft streaked toward London in a nearly three-hundred mile an hour descent. The right wing of the Mustang was now directly beneath the wing of the German rocket. The pilot gently brought up his right wing, bumping the wing of the flying bomb. He slightly turned the stick of his Mustang to the left; the wing of the streaking Mustang tipped the rocket's left wing up and to the right. The two craft separated in different directions.

By tipping the left wing of the rocket, the Mustang upset the guidance gyro of the V-1. The cruise missile immediately nosed over and headed straight down, spiraling its way into the cold water of the English Channel, exploding upon contact with the rough waters. The Londoners were safe from this bomb.

The Mustang briefly circled the rapidly descending rocket like a predatory bird. After the splash, the pilot began to ascend, and he looked around for any other V-1 rocket flames. Without seeing any other German cruise missiles, he sharply nosed the powerful Mustang upward at full throttle, rapidly accelerating to four hundred miles an hour to rejoin his flight group. The added force of the supercharger on the steep ascent threw the pilot back in his seat. The plane screamed upward, and on the adrenaline-charged ascent, the pilot looked to the heavens. He felt that he could continue the climb forever and chase the stars. His adrenaline coursed rapidly through his body. Life was good.

Risking a midair collision with the cruise missile, or worse, a premature bomb detonation, twenty-one year old Lieutenant Bill Cullerton had just "tipped" his first German V-1 buzz bomb into the drink, saving the lives of countless Londoners who would never even know it. As Bill rejoined his flight and made landfall on his way back to Steeple Morden, he looked down in the direction of the great city and thought about how much he would like to revisit London.

August 26, 1944

Ten days later, on another bomber mission, the 357th FS was released for a search and destroy strafing mission. Cullerton saw a German fighter preparing to land.

Bill was after a Focke-Wulfe 200, and he shot it up pretty well. The FW went up in flames and it was recorded as strafing kill, Bill's first. He went on to destroy a train in the same run, while three other guys took out some trains as well. The strafers shot up an aerodrome without any planes on the ground. They strafed radio towers and gun emplacements. It was a good day for the 357th.

By the end of August, Cullerton had learned a lot. After flying combat missions for only three months, he had tallied up two aerial victories, a strafing kill, two locomotives, and a V-2 buzz bomb. August was a costly month for the 355th FG, as they had lost twenty-eight Mustangs and several others that were beaten to scrap. The toll in pilots lost was extremely high: thirteen pilots had been killed or captured. Out of those thirteen, however, only two had been lost in air-to-air combat.

September 12, 1944

A month later, the 357th was flying bomber cover on a return mission over France when it engaged some fifty enemy fighters.

When the German fighters attacked, the bombers maintained close formation while the fighters dispersed. In the melee, Cullerton chased a German for quite some distance and it wasn't until the German fighter got away that Cullerton realized he had been completely separated from his group.

By great fortune, he met up with Havilland and Juntilla over the Schwarz military aerodrome. Cullerton and Havilland saw the field below with the parked German military aircraft all around. They coordinated their attack. Cullerton would pass from east to west and then loop back and pass from west to east, while Havilland would be doing the same, from north to south. Cullerton made six passes under fire, and Havilland got hit by ground fire on his second pass. Havilland broke off, but had already destroyed three aircraft on the ground. Juntilla made four passes, and he was also hit and damaged by ground fire. Juntilla managed four kills on the ground. Miraculously, Cullerton did not get hit on his strafing passes; nevertheless, in his six passes, as recorded by his gun camera, he destroyed seven aircraft on the ground. A total of fourteen German planes had been destroyed on the ground by three pilots, in only a matter of minutes.

Cullerton had set a new Eighth Air Force record and was now an official war hero. He was the first pilot in the entire Eighth AF to destroy seven planes in one day. Having been in England for only three and a half months, Cullerton already had two aerial kills and eight strafing kills. Ten Confirmed Kills made him a Double Ace. At the Eighth Air Force Headquarters (HQ), General Doolittle was given a report about the 357th FS action that had taken place that day.

From that day on, Bill had a fan in, none other than, General James Doolittle. Doolittle had a particular passion for "his" Strafers. He would be watching Bill and the other Strafers closely for the next nine months.

Americans Ambushed

Early October, 1944

The US B-17 bomber nicknamed *Crazy Mazie* dropped its bomb payload over Germany and turned back toward England. The bomber formation had been shot up before the bomb run, and they were somewhat scattered. The return trip would be another run through the gauntlet of German fighters.

The *Crazy Mazie* had just finished one half of her fourteenth mission. The pilot pushed the throttle all the way forward, and *Crazy Mazie* was on her way for a dash back to England. Twenty minutes into the return flight, the Luftwaffe jumped the returning B-17s. The *Mazie* was raked with twenty millimeter cannon fire from two Focke-Wulfe fighters. Her two inboard engines were on fire, and two of the crew members were dead. The *Mazie* lost altitude and dropped out of formation; she was in desperate trouble now. While the two FWs continued to attack, all of the available gunners on the fortress returned fire. The *Mazie* took more hits, and fuel was streaming from one of the wings. Her two inboard engines were out of commission. She was losing fuel, flying low, and flying slow.

The flight crew on board knew she wouldn't make it to a safe area in France, let alone England, so the navigator suggested Switzerland. The pilots banked left and headed straight toward the neutral country. The two FWs stayed with the bomber, peppering her with rounds as the besieged aircraft fought her way to Switzerland.

As the *Crazy Mazie* approached Switzerland, the FWs began to drift back and finally turn away. A cheer rose from the remaining bomber crewmembers as the bomber radioed England that they were in Switzerland, intact, and looking for a place to land. He added that they were damaged, but safe.

Given that the departing FWs had broken off to the right from the starboard side, the crew of the *Crazy Mazie* did not see two different aircraft fighters approach them from behind. The aircraft were located at the bombers' seven o'clock, the port side of the *Crazy Mazie*. The crew, not expecting an attack, was caught off guard when the Me 109s began driving murderous fire into the bomber. Part of her port wing broke away, and she lost trim. The *Mazie* nosed over, out of control, and headed straight down toward the Swiss countryside. The two pilots struggled to level her out, but she did not respond. The navigator's last words were a combination of horror and shock: "But we're in Switzerland!"

The *Crazy Mazie* and her crew vanished forever.

Steeple Morden

Fall 1944

It was 5:00 p.m. and dark outside. On its way out from Cambridge, The US Army jeep raced through Steeple Morden. Although it might be a bit too fast for the wet conditions, the jeep buzzed through the quiet village and out to the airbase of the 355th Fighter Group. Along with the driver were two officers: Major Willis and Major Price, both stoic types from Eighth Air Force HQ. These men were on a classified mission. The jeep approached the gate at the airbase.

"Papers, sir!" The gate guard examined the papers.

"Soldier, which way to the CO's office?"

"Take a right here, sir, all the way down, and it will be the last building on your right."

The guard handed the papers back to the driver and saluted. The jeep moved on.

Once the two visitors were inside of Lieutenant Colonel Cummings's office, the small airbase administration building was cleared for the confidential meeting between the base commander and the two majors from Eighth AF HQ.

Major Willis began as Price looked on.

"Colonel, this meeting never happened. We were never here."

The colonel nodded. "Go on," he uttered.

"We have reason to believe that someone," and he paused, "perhaps the Germans, has been shooting down some of our damaged bombers after they have reached the so-called safety of the Swiss border." The colonel looked on and Major Price took over.

"Sir, please read this letter and give it back to me."

Cummings read the letter twice and gave it back to the Major.

"Gentlemen," he began, "how can the 355th help?"

"Sir," began Price, "we will need two of your best available pilots to volunteer for this mission, and we must speak with them now."

Colonel Cummings picked up the phone and made the call. Within four minutes, Major John "Moon" Elder and First Lieutenant Bill Cullerton came into the office and stood at attention.

"At ease," said Cummings, and he continued, "Men, these officers are here from London and introductions are not necessary. We have a very unusual, very important, and very dangerous classified mission. If you accept it, as volunteers, mind you, you will be leaving at 0300, nine hours from now."

"But first," said Cummings, "once you leave on this mission, you are on your own. If something happens to you, and you end up where you shouldn't, well, the Army will have to protect itself at your expense. If you would like to think this over a bit, you have thirty seconds to do so."

The two pilots looked at each other and nodded. Both were at the end of their tours and would be going home shortly, but it didn't matter; they were hooked.

Elder and Cullerton volunteered for the mission and were both sworn to secrecy thereafter.

The lights were dimmed as cigarettes were lit and bourbon was poured, before Colonel Cummings began to lay out the mission.

The faint light in Lieutenant Colonel Cummings's office burned for another hour before the mysterious majors departed for Cambridge and back to London, or somewhere.

End of Tour

November 2, 1944

On November 2, 1944, the 355th FG sent up fifty-six Mustangs to roam at will, near Meersberg, Germany. Cullerton, as flight leader, spotted two Me 262 jet fighter aircraft. The German jet aircraft was the first of its kind and was a harbinger of things to come, jet power, the future of aviation. Cullerton and his flight went after the jets in full throttle with superchargers engaged, but the German jets simply outran the chasing Mustangs. After chasing the jets for quite a distance, the 357th found itself drawn into a large aerial engagement with German Focke-Wulfe and Messerschmitt fighters. Cullerton shot down two in the air, and their group descended on an aerodrome near Wernigerode and destroyed twenty-five more aircraft on the ground. In several coordinated passes, and under intense fire from the German defenses, Cullerton destroyed six more on the ground. In one day Cullerton destroyed eight enemy aircraft; Elder had a great day with one aerial kill and five on the ground; and Erickson destroyed six on the ground.

Cullerton had four aerial victories and fourteen strafing victories, making him the lead strafer in the entire Eighth Air Force at that time. He was determined to achieve Aerial Ace status with at least five "official" aerial combat victories. He knew he could destroy more on the ground to become a three-time Strafing Ace, but his active tour of duty was almost over.

Two days later, on November 4, 1944, his tour of duty was over. He had completed three hundred flying hours, or three hundred mission hours. At this point, the experienced pilots would rotate back to the States and teach new pilots who were coming up. Cullerton had done more than his share for the war effort, and the 355th FG wanted him back for an optional second tour. Cullerton was promised a promotion to captain and the opportunity to get that fifth aerial victory as well as teach new pilots. It was an honor and an offer he could not turn down. Cullerton was at the top of his game and couldn't conceive of finishing the war at a Texas air base. He would be back in January for his second tour, which would end in May, 1945. He wanted that fifth official aerial victory.

Payback for Mayzie

Mission Day

Elder and Cullerton ate breakfast alone the next morning. No one else was flying; in fact, most of the pilots were on leave and there wasn't any preflight prep for this mission.

Cullerton and Elder were considered two pilots with the proverbial "hot hand," since both had just completed their first tour with great attitude and impressive results; both had been "invited" back for a second tour of duty. Up until this mission, Elder had been a certified aerial ace with seven air victories, a strafing ace, as well as a record of destroying eight on the ground. Cullerton had four aerial victories, one short of aerial ace, but nearly a triple strafing ace, with fourteen destroyed on the ground. Colonel Cummings had chosen his volunteers wisely.

Out on the dark, chilly hardstand, amidst all of the parked and silent Mustangs, Cullerton and Elder's planes were the only ones warming up. Alone, and in a state of anticipation bordering on good old excitement, the two pilots taxied down the grass runway with fire snorting from the fuselage exhaust ports as they took off into the darkness.

After more than an hour of flight time, Cullerton and Elder's Mustangs reached their destination. As the sun rose, they patrolled at eighteen thousand feet above the far western border of Switzerland. They had circled above their rendezvous point for nearly an hour when they heard "Mayday" over their cockpit receivers. It was a wounded US bomber from far below. They slowly began their descent.

"Mayday, Mayday, Mayday. This is an American aircraft requesting assistance for Swiss landing coordinates and clearance. We are shot up and need landing coordinates, Mayday, Mayday, over."

"Mayday, Mayday . . ." and the pilot repeated the message again.

The bomber continued eastward for ten minutes as the two Mustangs kept the sun to their backs. They flew at ten thousand feet, trailing the bomber, which was flying at almost five thousand feet. Suddenly, two curiously marked Messerschmitt approached the bomber from the south and from behind. They were closing rapidly around five thousand feet above ground, the same elevation as the bomber. With superchargers engaged, the Mustangs nosed over and screamed earthward at nearly five hundred miles an hour. Elder then gave the order to turn on the gun cameras, which were engaged only when the firing trigger was active. Cullerton and Elder had to get an image of the air force markings on the Me 109s, before firing. That was why this mission was voluntary. The two Americans had to give away the element of surprise to determine, confirm, and record with their cameras whose fighters were shooting down Allied bombers over a neutral country.

But these two stealthy Me 109s were not German. They were Swiss Air Force Me 109s, and they began to fire their twenty millimeter cannon at the American bomber. The two Mustangs from Steeeple Morden quickly up the Swiss attack and the aerial engagement between the four fighters commenced. The experienced American pilots out flew and out fought the surprised Swiss pilots and it was all over very quickly. Elder and Cullerton each got one Swiss Me 109.

The planes were destroyed before the watchful eyes of the jubilant bomber crew as well as the Mustangs' gun cameras.

The bomber was on a "stalking horse" mission, sent to Switzerland via Germany from England with a full bomb payload to smoke out the culprits, who were suspected to be Swiss, but could have been German. The bomber had been sent courtesy of the 100th Bomb Group, the "Bloody 100th," and the two Mustangs had been sent courtesy of the 355th Fighter Group.

The Americans wanted to know if German Me 109s were violating neutral Swiss airspace by encroaching and then shooting down Allied bombers in Switzerland or whether, perhaps, it was the Swiss Air Force that might not be so neutral. Indeed, it *was* the Swiss Air Force who were shooting down the crippled Allied bombers over their neutral airspace.

Given that the two downed Me 109s were not German, the mission was not over. The bomber and their fighter escorts headed to the predetermined Swiss Air Force airfield. The American bomber dropped its payload from eight thousand feet and completely destroyed the Swiss Air Base and surrounding areas. The three American planes then headed for England. Mission accomplished.

After they had landed at Steeple Morden, the gun camera film from each Mustang was confiscated. No written record of the flight was ever made. Although each pilot had an aerial victory to his credit, it would never be officially counted. Cullerton's Ace-making, fifth aerial victory did not count. It never officially happened that day.

Cullerton's first tour was over, and the veteran pilot would soon be headed home for a two-month leave.

In the days that followed the mission that never happened, the military newspaper the *Stars and Stripes* issued an apology for an off-course bomber that accidentally bombed a Swiss airfield.

The United States and Britain never lost another wounded bomber over Switzerland again.

Home for Christmas

1944

Bill's trip home from England was going to be much different from his journey there. The Army bus took Bill and several other pilots to the bomber base at Bassingbourn. From there they would fly on a B-17 to Iceland and refuel. From Iceland, the B-17 would head for the East Coast of the United States, where Bill would contact his family and catch the next train to Chicago. If all went well, Bill could make it back to Chicago in seventy-two hours.

Before Bill left his base, he called home to let his family know that he would be back in November. Bill told his mother that he had been invited back for a second tour. As proud as she was, Ethel was not all that excited about it. Bill was unable to contact Steve, and he asked his mother to tell her about the second "invitation" to ease her into it.

As Cullerton sat in the B-17, bundled up and ready for his ride home with five other pilots and the rest of the cargo, he looked back on what had happened within that last week. The air and ground battle at Wernigerode had taken place a few days before, on November 2. There Bill had been credited with eight enemy aircraft destroyed. During the flight back to the base, he remembered thinking that he sure hoped his gun camera was working that day.

Bill knew that he had picked up several on the ground, but at the time he didn't know exactly how many.

The B-17 bounced through the pressure changes in the air as it ascended, and Cullerton's thoughts about his final mission on November 2 continued . . .

At this point, Bill was past the excitement of his successful mission, and he began to think about his meeting with the film reviewers who certified all of the pilots' claims after the mission films and discussions were completed.

"Lieutenant, we have reviewed your film, and you had a great day yesterday."

"Thank you, sir. Do you have the results?"

Yes, Lieutenant. Your two aerial kills are confirmed and we are giving you a credit for six more on the ground. That makes a total of eight for the day, and we believe it is another Eighth Air Force record."

The officer had not quite completed the discussion; he hadn't dismissed Cullerton, so Bill seized the opportunity to ask a question. "Sir, is there something else?"

"Look, Lieutenant, we could have probably given you two or three more on the ground, but we are going to certify six on the ground. Eight in one day breaks your old record of seven."

At the time, Cullerton had been elated about eight, but now that he had had time to think about it, it started to bother him, as he thought to himself, *If they gave me ten instead of eight, well, maybe that sounded like too many, too unbelievable. It must be true, otherwise they wouldn't have mentioned it to me.*

His thoughts about the numbers trailed off. He was content with the number eight and was happy to be going home.

When he arrived in New Jersey, Bill couldn't get hold of anyone, so he decided to make a surprise arrival. At 8:00 p.m. his train arrived at Union Station in Chicago; Bill hopped into a cab and took it back to his home on the West Side. Instead of walking in, Bill rang the doorbell.

When Ethel opened the door, she was shocked to see her son standing in the doorway. Bill's dad was home, and they called Jean at school. They celebrated that night and looked forward to having a great Thanksgiving dinner this year.

There was still somebody Bill had yet to see; his parents knew that he was anxious, so Orville tossed him the car keys and Bill was off to Oak Park.

Still dressed in his uniform, he turned down Wesley Street and pulled up in front of Steve's house. He grabbed his cap and bouquet of flowers and headed up to the front door. He rang the bell and waited. Through the faceted glass on the front door, he saw a figure walking toward him. Steve didn't wear a man's suit, so it must be Ralph approaching the front door. As Bill straightened up and cleared his throat, Mr. Stephen opened the door and extended his hand to Bill.

"Glad you're home, son; glad you're home." Bill was pleased to hear the man's voice. Mr. Stephen called upstairs, "Elaine, Elaine! There's a package here for you!"

Mr. Stephen turned back and winked at Bill. Elaine emerged from her room onto the landing and looked down into the foyer. In complete astonishment, she exclaimed, "Bill!" and descended quickly into the foyer, where the two embraced each other. Mr. Stephen smiled broadly, as did Steve's mother, who came into the room as well.

Bill and Steve spent a lot of time together, and the time passed quickly. They had no choice but to have Thanksgiving dinner twice. Things were different back home this year. The tide of the war had turned in 1944, in both the European and Pacific theaters of battle. America and Great Britain had invaded the continent of Europe, and the United States was taking back the islands in the Pacific. The Allied

Forces were moving closer to Berlin and Tokyo. The Thanksgiving holiday had even greater meaning this year.

The newspapermen knew that Bill was coming home after his tour, and they caught up with Bill, who was happy to oblige them. He helped to write articles about his experiences in Europe for the *Chicago Times* and the *Chicago Tribune*. The papers interviewed Elaine, as well. The one-time boy Mayor of Chicago, turned war hero, was asked to promote war bonds on several occasions in and around Chicago, and he gladly agreed as part of his civil and patriotic duty.

In mid-December, Bill and Steve went downtown to do some shopping, along with hundreds of other things in Chicago. State Street was never more exciting to Bill than it was that year. They checked out the Marshall Field's and Carson Pirie Scott Christmas window displays down the block on State Street. Goldblatt's, Montgomery Ward's, and Sears Roebuck all bustled with activity. Salvation Army carolers and bell ringers were on every corner. It was snowing, and Christmas lights in the loop were wonderful to see. Bill appreciated everything more now than ever before. Arm in arm, the two walked everywhere together.

Bill and Steve only separated once that day, to buy each other's Christmas gifts. Steve went one way and Bill headed the other, in the direction of a jewelry store located on Wabash Avenue.

Later that day, Bill and Steve went to dinner at the Walnut Room Restaurant, near the Marshall Field's Christmas tree, upstairs in the great department store. They hadn't talked much about it, but Steve decided to ask the question. "So, Bill . . . tell me about your invitation to fly a second tour."

Bill had known that question would come sooner or later, and was quite surprised that it had taken her a few weeks to mention it. As she waited for a response, Steve glared at him like a German flak gunner, he was sure. Bill was twitching and Steve was enjoying it. She wasn't angry that Bill had signed up for a second tour, but rather she was worried. She knew that the longer he flew the better the odds were that something could happen to him, especially since Bill was such an aggressive pilot.

"Well . . ." Bill uttered.

"Yes?"

"Boy, doesn't this Christmas tree look great this year, Steve?"

"Take your medicine, Cullerton. You are not dodging this one," said Steve.

"Steve, they asked me back, which is an honor, and I couldn't refuse. They promised to promote me to captain. I don't think I could live with myself if I declined the offer, regardless of how many planes I already got."

Little did Bill know that Steve had been prepared for this for a long time.

"Relax, I understand. I know you well enough."

"I'll be home in May, for sure."

"When you are not here, May is a long time away. My life is day to day when you are gone," Steve revealed.

"The good news is that I don't go back to England until mid-January."

Bill and Elaine toasted to that and had a great dinner beneath the Marshall Field's Christmas tree.

The Best Laid Plans

December 18, 1944

Bill woke up early this morning in his bed at home, where he hadn't slept for two and a half years. He lay in his bed and stared at the bedroom walls and his dresser, admiring all of his things that he still had from high school. He decided that it was time to put all of those things away. As he continued to lie there, his mother called him from downstairs, in a serious voice, so Bill threw on a shirt and rushed down.

Ethel and Orville had read the newspaper headlines and the lead story; now they turned on the radio. The Germans had begun a major offensive in the Ardennes forest. They were counterattacking the Allies. Their swift attack, with over eight hundred thousand soldiers and one thousand tanks, had caught the Americans and the British by surprise. The Germans had surrounded and cut off two US regiments, which had been forced to surrender. The great German breakout winter battle had begun. The newspapers said that American servicemen who were home on leave were being ordered to return to duty. All leave was cancelled. Bill called the regional command for confirmation and learned that he would be back in Europe before Christmas Day. Bill called Steve right away.

"Steve, I'm going back to England, the Germans have."

"I know, Bill, my parents just told me. The radio is on. When will you leave, exactly?"

"I'm not sure; I've got to make a few more calls to find out. I'll let you know, but I think tonight may be my last night home for a while. Can I come by your house later?"

"Yes, call me and let me know when you're coming."

"All right. Bye, Steve."

"Goodbye, Bill."

Bill made a few calls and found out that he needed to leave as soon as possible. While he packed his gear and put on his uniform, his mother checked the train schedule. Because of the urgency of the return to battle, extra trains were being added after midnight, for military only.

Ethel, Orville, and Jean drove Bill over to Elaine's house and dropped him off there. They all said their goodbyes in front of the Stephen house. Before they drove away, Bill reassured everyone that he would see them in May.

Bill and Steve sat around the Stephens' Christmas tree to exchange their gifts. Bill opened Elaine's gift first. IT was a sterling silver St. Christopher medal. "For your safety, Bill."

"Thanks, Steve, I will keep it on through the end of the war" as he slipped it over his head. I have one for you here somewhere," he said as he shuffled through his belongings. "Here it is. You can open it now." It was a tiny box.

Bill pulled the gift out from his duffle bag and handed it over to Elaine. She stared at it and looked at Bill with a puzzled expression.

"Oh, Bill . . ."

"Steve, will you marry me?"

"But Bill, you said not until after the war."

"I know, I know," he cut in, "but I'll be home in May. I promise I won't let them get me."

Elaine looked at Bill and smiled, "Of course I'll marry you. You nut; I would have married you two years ago!"

They both laughed a good long laugh and sat on the couch together for the rest of the evening. Mr. Stephen drove them both to the train station downtown, around midnight. There wasn't much talking on the ride there, but Bill and Elaine held hands the entire way.

Like a culprit traveling to the gallows, Bill felt the quickness of the ride downtown. Bill shook Mr. Stephen's hand and thanked him for the ride. The newly engaged couple held each other for a while. After their goodbye kiss, Bill looked at Steve and her father and said, "I'll be back in May; I will see you in May."

With that, Bill walked from the curb and toward the station into which many other soldiers were headed. He turned back and waved before passing through the doors. Elaine, standing next to the car, waved back. When Bill had walked into the building, she looked around. The scene was like a Depression-era kissing contest in every direction.

Second Tour

January 1945

Cullerton's second tour of duty had started a month early as a result of the surprise counterattack by the Germans in the Ardennes forest that December. The massive German counteroffensive would become known as the Battle of the Bulge. The Germans had attacked fifty-five thousand British and five hundred thousand Americans who were stretched very thinly along the entire Western Front, in an effort to break through to the North Sea port city of Antwerp, in Belgium, and split the British and American Allies in two. The German plan was to force a stalemate long enough to seek terms for peace with the United States and Britain. The Germans attacked to the west with six hundred thousand soldiers in two armies, which included twenty-nine divisions. Included in this surprise winter assault were divisions of SS Infantry and SS tank divisions. It was the atrocities committed by the Sixth Panzer Army, First SS Division, against an overwhelmed and surrendering Allied convoy of lightly armed artillery observers during the battle that would later fuel a fire of revenge and retribution against the Germans by the Allies.

Cullerton, along with other pilots and soldiers who had been on leave, were recalled for the Allied counteroffensive. The men flew back to England to remain there through the end of December. The recalled pilots and airmen in England took express military trains back to Cambridge, and transport vehicles hurried them back to their respective bases. Once there, the returning GIs were informed of the details of the enemy offensive. Throughout the month of January, details of the scope of the entire German attack and the slaughtering of surrendering American soldiers at Malmedy began to emerge. The SS had executed 88 American POWs instead of sending them to POW camps. Word also spread about resistance of the surrounded Americans at Bastogne, Belgium. Since the Germans could not occupy it, Bastogne became the first domino in the collapse of the month-long, powerful German counteroffensive, known to the Germans as Operation Wacht am Rhein, or Watch on the Rhine.

By Christmas, as the weather cleared, the soldiers holding out Bastogne had been supported and reinforced with supplies of food, clothing, weapons, and ammunition by the Eighth AF. Once again, air power played a key role in turning the tide of battle.

Cullerton and other veteran pilots found themselves performing many roles upon their return to England. They were, at once, instructors to the new pilots and flight leaders. Cullerton flew bomber support missions as well as supply drops in the Ardennes forest. Although Bill had had second thoughts about another tour, he knew he had made the right decision to return as soon as the Battle of the Bulge started.

Throughout January and February of 1945, the Allied fighters flew bomber cover missions that took them deeper into Germany. A squadron was made up of fighters like Bill Cullerton and Bob Garlich and was released to strafe. The Dragon Squadron of Steeple Morden hunted with a vengeance; the 357th tore up anything in the German infrastructure they could find. Their earnestness was fueled by duty, of course, but the pilots fought with a higher intensity due to the emergence of the Nazi executions of surrendered Allied soldiers.

The executions of at Malmedy were a dark harbinger of things to come.

Sometimes the Mustangs were bombers. Over German-occupied towns, which were poised and waiting for the Allied advance on the ground, the Mustangs carried a five-hundred-pound bomb under each wing. The Mustangs circled the towns, looking for enemy tank emplacements. German Tiger tanks and Panzer tanks were either stationed or motoring the streets. When the tanks were spotted, pilots lined up, swept in low, and released the bombs from thirty feet in the air. These bombs had incredible forward momentum and would skip, or bounce, down the street until they slammed into the tanks or an occupied building and explode. "Skip" bombing was devastating to the enemy.

Without firing a shot, the strafers would clip telephone wires with their wings to cut off German communications. This held effective until the Germans strung up steel cables around the telephone wires. In any attempt to clip, the wing of an airplane would be completely torn off. The Allies had to change strategy, as the tactics from both sides continued to escalate.

With six .50 caliber machine guns firing at once, a Mustang strafing pilot could annihilate anything. Instead of clipping the wires, a Mustang would destroy the poles used to string the steel cable. If the Germans were using wireless communications, the Mustangs would destroy the towers and buildings that were transmitting the signals, as well as the military gun emplacements surrounding the towers.

Strafing was a perilous way to fight. One bullet from an infantryman's rifle could cut an engine cooling line, and the plane could be lost. A well-aimed shot could kill the pilot. These instances occurred, and they happened all too often. Four out of every five of the Allied fighter pilots in the war in Europe were downed while strafing. It was dangerous, but the strafers kept coming.

Any enemy train was fair game. Strafers would have to first shoot up the tracks under the locomotive to stop the train, then loop around and start shooting the railcars that followed. The results were obvious: there were fewer reinforcements to stop the Allied advance, less fuel for the Panzer and Tiger tanks, fewer weapons with which to fight, and of course, with a destroyed train, now-useless tracks. Mustangs and P-47 Thunderbolts strategically cut up railroad marshalling yards with guns and bombs.

Railway marshalling yards were a preferred target for bombing by the Allied bomber fleets, but the Germans were extremely resourceful in making the yards operational again. Strafers followed up heavy bombing missions with pinpoint destruction of the main switching areas. The strafers were sent in to destroy the locomotives, railcars, tracks, and switching stations and towers that had been missed during high-altitude bombing, to help keep the Germans from moving vital resources to the front lines.

The Germans were exceptional at concealing anti-aircraft weapons in the forests. If it was suspected that the Germans were concealed in a specific forested area, the strafers would be sent in with a new type of bomb release. The new bomb, the napalm bomb, contained an incendiary that sent a flaming jellylike gasoline substance in all directions when it exploded. The sticky substance would continue to burn after the explosion, allowing strafers to burn the forest and the enemy out of its cover.

Above all, the preferred strafing targets were the German aerodromes of the Luftwaffe. The aerodromes were spread out over rural areas and heavily guarded by anti-aircraft gun emplacements. The emplacements would be concealed in the thick tree cover near the airfields, or in heavily sandbagged or fortified enclosures on or around the airfields. The strafers continued to hit these targets whether there were gun emplacements or not.

During Cullerton's first tour, an attacking Mustang was damaged on an airfield-strafing mission. The pilot was Captain Bert Marshall of the 354th FS. Marshall landed his plane safely behind enemy lines in German-held territory, as his engine failed due to a damaged cooling system. Marshall's wingman, Lieutenant Royce Priest, landed his undamaged P-51 nearby to pick up the stranded Marshall. Marshall strongly insisted that Priest get out of there, but Priest wouldn't leave his friend. Cullerton, Spencer, and Crandell continued to circle above the grounded pilots, making sure they were safe. The three pilots strafed everything that moved as the Germans began to close in on Priest and Marshall. Miraculously, both pilots crammed into Priest's cockpit, and with Marshall sitting on Priest's lap, they were able to take off. Marshall took control of the stick and speed, while Priest worked the pedals. The men made it back to Steeple Morden with Cullerton, Spencer, and Crandell in escort. It was a courageous move by Royce Priest, and he was awarded the Silver Star for his bravery.

A Good Fight

It was a sunny day in March. It was always sunny when the 357th FS, or anyone else for that matter, flew twenty-eight thousand feet above the clouds. Cullerton led a squadron of Mustangs to patrol the skies. The flight was scheduled to rendezvous with a bomber group that had yet to appear. Since Cullerton had begun his second tour, he had added several strafing kills to his total aircraft kill count, but he hadn't gotten his fifth aerial victory yet. He was getting anxious, as his second tour was almost up.

Through the piercing rays of the sun, one of the element leaders spotted a pack of nearly twenty German Focke-Wulfe fighters in the distance. The German gaggle was below Cullerton's flight and in front of the American group, headed in the same direction. If Cullerton's group began to attack now, they would come out of the sun to approach the Germans from above and behind with the element of surprise. Cullerton issued the attack strategy so that each of his element leaders knew which enemy fighter to pursue. As flight leader himself, Cullerton would be taking on the German flight leader.

Cullerton led the dive down from twenty eight thousand feet to twenty thousand feet, where the Germans were patrolling. As he dove down, zeroing in on the flight leader, Cullerton's speed increased to nearly four hundred eighty miles an hour. His senses were heightened as his adrenaline began to rush, and his heart thumped against his rib cage. Cullerton was engaging a multiple ace, a veteran German pilot and a colonel. He closed in on the leader too rapidly, so he cut the throttle and extended the wing flaps in order to increase the drag on the plane. Trying to slow down quickly, he realized that he was going to fly right past the German leader with his sturdy forward momentum. He matched the German's speed; the two leaders were now flying neck and neck. Each looked at the other, this was a rare encounter, and it was a first for Cullerton. As he looked over, he saw numerous strike marks on the tail of the Focke-Wulfe, each a kill mark. Conversely, the German colonel had noticed the twenty-plus victory swastikas on Cullerton's plane and smiled. The battle was on, at fifteen thousand feet above Germany.

Cullerton took the colonel by surprise. Since he was able to slow down and slip behind the German, Cullerton won the first move. With the Mustang behind him, the colonel didn't panic, but instead he began to take evasive measures. He snap-rolled the highly maneuverable FW 190 to the left and dove deep. Cullerton dove after it, firing all six guns at once. The FW went into a tight turn to the left to shake off the Mustang, but Cullerton reacted well enough to stay with him. He couldn't get an inside shot on the FW; the German pilot was too good. At the same time, Cullerton's wingman kept the colonel's wingman busy, allowing the one-on-one battle to continue. All of the other FWs and Mustangs were engaged. This had become a classic dogfight, where thirty-six planes were flying in all directions.

The FW pulled into a tight climb, an unexpected move from the German, since the Mustang could outclimb the FW. The colonel was trying to loop back on his tail; Cullerton had to act fast, pulling his plane into a high climb. The Mustang screamed around, staying with the FW's turning radius. Cullerton kept the Mustang in a tight circle and settled on the FW's tail. The German couldn't shake the Mustang, but Cullerton couldn't get a shot on the FW either.

The one-on-one engagement was a standoff. Cullerton was nearly out of ammo, and fuel consumption was becoming a concern, as he still had to get back to England. He was going to have to break off the engagement.

Ahead of the Mustang, the FW continued to roll and shift from left to right at extremely high speeds. The German knew that the American was good; his plan was to keep the American off balance, break off the engagement, and escape in the opposite direction. The colonel knew how to waste American ammunition.

A frustrated Cullerton knew the colonel would have to break off soon as well. His instincts took over. Cullerton, a left-handed man, knew that most pilots were right-handed; therefore many controlled the stick with their right hand while flying. He also knew that the natural movement of a pilot was to pull back on the stick with the right hand, drawing the plane upward and slightly to the right. Bill anticipated the German to be right-handed, so he backed off and moved slightly to the left of the FW. When the Mustang drifted left, the colonel took the bait and began to break right. Cullerton pulled up on his stick, hit the rudder, skidded to the right and fired the rest of his ammunition ahead of the FW where he anticipated the German would go.

The German broke to the right and into Cullerton's bullet stream. The FW burst into pieces, and Cullerton watched as the German bird fell from the sky. He banked the Mustang to avoid the explosion; as he looked back, he saw no sign of the pilot bailing.

Cullerton was the last to join the group, and they escorted the bombers back to England. Mercifully, the rest of the flight was uneventful. He reflected on his victory. It had lasted only a few minutes, but the intensity of it had made it seem like an hour.

The engagement with the German flight leader provided him the well-deserved fifth aerial victory and Aerial Ace status, in addition to his multiple Strafing Ace achievements. He had achieved his goals and done his job well for Uncle Sam.

The Strafing Mission at Ansbach, Germany

April 8, 1945

The two Mustangs saw the German aerodrome ahead, surrounded by German fighter planes. Flight leader Captain Bill Cullerton barked out the attack plan as the two American P-51D Mustangs zeroed in for a strafing attack.

"I'll make the first pass north to south; Bob, you follow east to west."

"Roger that, Flight Leader."

With that, Cullerton nosed his Mustang down, leveling off at about fifty feet above the ground and traveling at two hundred miles an hour as he began to strafe the German aircraft on the runway. He destroyed one plane and sent a second one into flames. Cullerton's plane bucked, taking a direct hit in the fuselage right behind the pilot's seat, from a twenty millimeter anti-aircraft cannon concealed in the trees. The plane exploded. As Lieutenant Bob Garlich began his own strafing pass, he heard the explosion and looked over to see Cullerton's plane erupt with flames. Garlich pulled up as he took several machine gun hits; he was losing fuel. As he looked around again for Cullerton's plane, he saw that Cullerton was gone. Garlich couldn't believe it. He had seen yet another strafing pilot killed in action.

Alone with a broken radio and a plane leaking fluids, Garlich had one option, which was to head toward home and only hope that he could make it. Back at the base in Steeple Morden, England, Garlich was going to have to break the news about Cullerton.

Inside the Mustang, Cullerton's gun camera had recorded two strafing kills. The two hundred millimeter cannon shell had hit his plane on the left side of the fuselage, and the twenty millimeter round had hit the auxiliary fuel, which exploded in the rear of the cockpit. It was a steel plate behind Cullerton's seat that saved him while he was still inside the burning aircraft. He pulled up on the stick to gain altitude; it was instinct to go for altitude while traveling at one hundred eighty miles per hour so close to ground. The plane lost power as it ascended; Cullerton popped the canopy and jumped. The plane was only two hundred feet above the ground, not high enough for his parachute to save him, but he didn't have a choice: he had to get out of the plane.

The fireball began to descend as the small human figure emerged and began to tumble forward into the sky.

Cullerton tugged the ripcord on his parachute as he soared through the air at one hundred fifty miles an hour. The forward momentum popped the chute open and he immediately descended. He crash-landed on the ground, hitting his backside, and tumbled. He was in serious pain, but against all odds he had just beaten death twice within a matter of ninety seconds. His luck was holding. He hadn't suffered any broken bones, so he grabbed his survival kit, checked to make sure he had his knife and the Army-issue Colt .45, and quickly tried to recover his bearings.

He landed in a clearing on the edge of a forest. Bill was at the eastern edge of the great and ominous Black Forest of southern Germany. He ran one way to ditch his chute, in an attempt to confuse any chasers, and then he headed the other way, to the west, and into the cover of the dense Black Forest.

**SCHEMATIC POSITIONS OF ALLIED & GERMAN ARMIES
ON 4/8/45** (The day Cullerton was shot down.)

 **GERMAN CONTROLLED
TERRITORY**

Bill quickly approached the tree line on the southeastern edge of the forest. In he went, stopping only to see if the Germans had seen him. The posse of German soldiers was large enough to split into multiple directions, and one of those groups began to head right for him. Cullerton, who had spent most of his summers living in the great Northwoods of Wisconsin hunting, camping, and fishing, was now being chased into the great Black Forest of south Germany.

He ditched his flight overgear under a pine tree. He was wearing his brown wool clothes and the fur-lined leather jacket without any US markings on it. He checked his survival kit, which contained two chocolate bars, a water cup with halazone water-purification pills, Benzedrine pills to stay awake, a compass, some matches, his knife, and of course, his Army-issue Colt 45 pistol. He checked the clip; it was full plus had one in the chamber, but he couldn't find the second clip. Knowing that he only had eight shots, he realized he couldn't waste a single bullet. Cullerton held the gun up before his face and looked at it; a chill ran down his spine. The underbrush crackled beneath the footsteps of approaching German soldiers, and suddenly Cullerton, who was now perhaps seventy miles deep inside of dangerous and deadly Nazi Germany, switched into survival mode.

Back near the Ansbach Aerodrome, the shell of Cullerton's Mustang lay smoldering in the green turf. It had come down quickly and was still somewhat identifiable. The young German soldiers who had shot the "dragon" down inspected their handiwork with a sense of accomplishment. Civilians and soldiers went to the wreckage to gloat, and if necessary, to kill the bastard flier who came to kill them. What a strange visage this was: villagers with pitchforks milling around the hulk of the great aircraft. There would be no execution today, however, for the dragon pilot was not to be seen. After forty-five minutes or so, the civilians began to disperse; a couple of soldiers lingered. The SS officer on the scene noticed the swastikas on the side of the airplane; he knew the symbols of the different Fighter Groups and recognized the dragon symbol of the 357th Fighter Squadron. The officer was aware that his troops had brought down an aircraft of a Steeple Morden strafer. The pilot had escaped, but not for long.

Colonel Friedrich Gunther Gruber would see to it that the American was caught and summarily executed. Gruber stood there in his black-and-silver SS uniform; no one approached him, simply because they were afraid of him. The lights had gone out in Gruber's eyes years ago, and as he stared at the wreckage, he had the look of someone who had lost his soul. Either the British or Americans, Gruber wasn't sure who, had killed most of his family in bombing raids. He thought it was probably the British, but it didn't really matter. Gruber hated both adversaries anyway, since his younger brother, Erwin, had been killed the previous summer during the Normandy invasion. Erwin Gruber had been a lieutenant in the regular Germany Army, and the two brothers had been close. Colonel Friedrich Gruber of the German Waffen SS continued to stare at the wreckage of the *Miss Steve* P-51 Mustang. He didn't have any illusions about the outcome of the war, but for Gruber it was personal, and he would do everything he could to catch and kill the American who had attacked his command at Ansbach. At this point in the War, an SS officer could do just about anything he wanted to do inside Germany, and killing this American was what Gruber intended to do.

Postflight at Steeple Morden

Sunday April 8, 1945, 2:45 p.m.
Steeple Morden

By mid afternoon, Lieutenant Garlich and the rest of the 357th Fighter Squadron had made it back to base at Steeple Morden. Garlich, very disheartened, reported once again that Cullerton's plane had exploded and he had not seen a parachute anywhere. Barring the lieutenant's return, a telegram would be set in motion to notify the Cullerton family back in Chicago that their son, Captain William J. Cullerton, had been officially listed as Missing in Action (MIA) on this day, April 8, 1945. Until the military received additional confirmation regarding Cullerton's status, dead or captured, the War Department would issue a Missing in Action announcement. That message would be devastating for the family, as it always was, but at least an MIA telegram would soften the blow and help prepare the Cullerton family and Steve for the expected and inevitable telegram: Killed in Action.

Unfortunately for the Cullerton family and Bill's fiancé, the *Chicago Times* and *Chicago Tribune* war correspondents who had followed Cullerton's heroics had quickly reported this terrible turn of events for the top ace in Chicago.

The brass at Steeple Morden knew that the Chicago newspapers would report the loss of Cullerton well before the Army officially would be able to. It was determined that someone there would call Cullerton's family before they read about it in the newspaper. During an early afternoon in England, the call to Chicago was made.

So close to the end of the war, and for such a highly decorated pilot, this was a call that Colonel Claiborne Kinnard did not want to make.

The phone rang just as Ethel Cullerton was leaving for Sunday morning Mass.

"Hello . . . Is this the Orville Cullerton residence?" began Colonel Kinnard.

"Yes, it is. This is Ethel Cullerton speaking. Who is this?"

"Ma'am, are you Captain Bill Cullerton's mother?"

"Yes, sir. Who is this?"

"This is Colonel Kinnard calling from England. Ma'am, I regret to inform you that Captain Cullerton has gone Missing in Action today."

"I—I—wait, excuse me, s-sir—is Bill okay? Is he alive?"

"Ma'am, we don't know for sure, but it is possible. He is behind enemy lines and perhaps a prisoner. We just don't know yet."

Ethel sat down, her shoulders drooped; she continued to speak with the colonel.

"What happened, Colonel?" she asked.

"All I can tell you, ma'am, is that his plane was hit by ground fire."

"Is my son alive, Colonel? Please!" she leaned her head into the palm of her hand,

"It is possible, ma'am."

"Sir, do you think he's alive?"

Kinnard paused a moment. He believed Cullerton's chances for survival were close to zero. The colonel wanted to give the family some hope, at least for now.

"Ma'am, it is possible that he is alive, so we are listing him as Missing in Action. I wanted to let you know before you heard elsewhere. An Army staff car will stop by your house this afternoon and you will receive a formal telegram from the War Department listing your son as MIA. There is hope, Mrs. Cullerton."

"Thank you, sir . . . for calling me personally. Will you call if you get any word from Bill?"

"Mrs. Cullerton, I would be more than happy to make that phone call. In the meantime, I am very sorry."

"Thank you for calling."

"Goodbye, ma'am."

Ethel feared the Army knew more than they were telling her. She dropped the phone out of her hand, and her chin sinking into her chest, she began to cry. The blue star in the Cullerton front window would remain blue.

Into the Black Forest

April 8, 1945
Day 1 on the Run

The German soldiers continued to search throughout the forest. The further into the pine they went, the darker it became. A pair of young privates had gone deep enough in so that they would not be seen from the clearing beyond. Here, they began to delay their search. The two privates stopped alongside a sweeping pine and decided to take watch from there. They stood by quietly, waiting for any sudden movements, and they fired multiple shots in the direction of any noise.

Cullerton, now in survival mode, glanced around without moving his head. He knew that one move or even the snap of a twig meant his death. Through the branches he could see a finger, tapping on its rifle trigger. *Itchy trigger finger*, he thought. The only thing that Cullerton could do now was to wait. *This guy is ready to shoot. No motion, light breathing, and don't close the eyes. Oh, hell, what if I have to sneeze?* He was curled around the tree trunk, leaning on his right elbow and clutching his 45 in his left hand. It didn't take long for him to lose feeling in his right arm. *Ohhh, the tingling.* He winced and flexed his arm muscles in hopes of relieving some pain.

Twenty minutes had gone by; as Cullerton remained motionless, he felt a strange tickling sensation on his hand. He looked down and saw a hideous spider. It stopped at the base of his thumb, where it bit him, not once but twice. *This damn German spider. It has to be a Nazi spider*, he thought. Cullerton watched it walk off his hand and back onto the forest floor, leaving his hand itchy and throbbing. It took all of his power to let the furry bastard escape, but Bill dared not move.

After forty-five minutes of lingering around Cullerton's tree, the soldiers finally left. They had had enough and were ready to head back, since daylight was fading. Cullerton could finally breathe and, at last, scratch his hand. He stretched a bit under the tree and stayed where he was until nightfall. After dark he would move with great speed through the Black Forest, toward the Allied lines.

Eight German soldiers returned to the Ansbach Airfield and reported that the American was nowhere to be found. Colonel Gruber expected to hear as much, as he had already issued orders for a special tracking team, the Schutzstaffel protection squadron (SS), to pursue the American. Gruber wanted to go after Cullerton himself, along with two sharpshooters and his three best trackers. The American would have a twenty-four hour head start on Gruber's team, but it wasn't enough time to escape the special trackers. A cold, downturned smile shone briefly on Gruber's face. These trackers were a specially trained breed, trained to track humans, and once they caught them, they would tear their prey to pieces. These giant malevolent monsters were bred for size, ferocity, and tracking abilities. It was a new breed of German killer hunting dogs, a cross between an Irish wolfhound, a German giant schnauzer, and a Rottweiler, a combination of size, tracking tenacity, and jaw power. These dogs were trained to kill gypsies, Jews, and criminals.

Bill had no idea of what was in pursuit of him. If he had, he might not have waited until dark to begin his journey through the forest. In fact, he half convinced himself that the Germans had given up the search. Well, he could at least hope they had given up.

Still hopeful, deeper into the ancient forest the young pilot went. What originally felt like an escape began to feel more like a nightmare. After an hour of moving swiftly, he realized that the darkness had become complete. He could no longer see his hand in front of his face in this obsidian world. While he was trying to dodge trees, Bill crashed his head into the outstretched branch of a large oak tree; he went down, seeing stars and feeling the rapid pulse of blood in his ears. He knelt on the forest floor and waited for the stars to disappear.

"This evasion effort," he whispered to himself, "is off to a rough start." He had been moving toward the west quickly for a couple of hours, which had put distance between him and Ansbach. Given his current disadvantaged location, behind enemy lines, he thought it would be a good time to rest and assess the situation. As he tried to clear his head, he lit up a match to read his compass so that he could get his westerly heading precise. As he read the glowing dials, he realized that he was traveling slightly off course. He took inventory of his survival items. These items, the clothes on his back, and the skills he had learned from both the military and his experience in the Wisconsin Northwoods, were all Bill had. He needed to travel on foot about seventy miles to make the Allied front lines. He shrugged; in complete darkness he sat still and listened. He heard noises in the distance, movements. Human? Was it an animal? His senses were sharp; his pulse began to race as he vainly searched the darkness with his eyes. Nothing. He knew he had to continue through the forest.

Bill considered what stood between him and freedom, or at least safety. The pilots and aircrews had been bombing Germany for three years, and many of the German civilian population hated Allied airmen. Every so often, Allied crews were taken prisoner and there were reports of beatings and executions. He had no intention of being caught or taking his chances with the Germans.

Even though the war was only weeks from being over, he couldn't risk contact with German civilians. He would have to stay out of sight, steal, or rather, "liberate" food when he could, and keep heading west. Temperatures dropped below freezing during the early spring weather, and he wasn't able to build a fire. He would have to take the Benzedrine pills to stay awake at night. If the Germans didn't get him, the weather still could. He would sleep in short stints as much as possible and improvise as he went along. Some German soldiers were retreating and some were deserting. In either case, he did not want to bump into them or the Home Guard, which was an armed quasi-military group made up of men that were too old and boys that were too young for the regular army. The combat arm of the SS, which was known as the Waffen SS, was quasi-German military and a group unto itself; it did not report to regular German Army Command. The Waffen SS was unlike anyone's regular military, including Germany's regular army.

The SS began as security for the Nazi political party; however, by the end of WWII, the SS would add a military arm to its security duties and transform itself into a highly sophisticated fighting force. The Waffen SS became such a machine of terror that even the Wehrmacht, or regular German Army, feared its wrath. The Waffen SS contained several divisions of SS soldiers who were godless; they fought fiercely, mercilessly, and took no prisoners. By the end of World War II, the SS had become so large that it had several branches, each having its own unique brand of horror. Since the SS was not a national organization, but merely a political party's entourage, much like the Roman praetorian guard, the SS did not adhere to any international rules of engagement.

By 1920, Adolf Hitler had found his way to the top of the National Socialist German Workers' Party. Hitler's values and beliefs were so defined by hate and anti-Semitism that it became necessary to form a protection squad to quell any saboteurs that stood in the way of his party. By 1929, Heinrich Himmler had been appointed Reichsfuhrer, or commander of the SS. The National Socialist, or Nazi, party was not the first political party to have its own security force. According to Himmler, who had been raised Roman Catholic, the armed SS man was to be godless and belong to a special brotherhood of knights whose roots went back to pagan Germania. Furthermore, it was considered 'un-German' to believe in the Christian message of reconciliation and tolerance. Silver skulls of death pinned to members' hats or uniform lapels gave a clear signal to the observer that mercy or benevolence would not be found within the person wearing the SS uniform. This cold message is somewhat evident in the intimidating all-black uniforms trimmed in silver SS that earned the SS the ridiculous nickname of the Black Angels.

Different SS groups carried out various types of operations. The Totenkopfterven SS, or Death's Head SS, ran and oversaw the Nazi concentration camps. Another wing of the SS was the Panzer Division of the Waffen SS. The Panzer Armored Division became infamous for its part in the Malmedy Massacre of US prisoners of war that took place during the Battle of the Bulge, when nearly one hundred American POWs were ordered into an open field at the side of a road and gunned down by Waffen SS soldiers, instead of being sent to a German prisoner of war camp. The bodies of the dead Americans were then used as target practice for any Waffen SS that passed the killing field.

A somewhat forgotten arm of the SS was a group called der Werwolf. The werewolves were SS men dressed in plain clothes who found most of their action when invading armies entered Germany at the end of the war. Der Werwolfe committed acts of terror, such as bombing buildings, killing collaborators, and sniping, in an effort to preserve Nazism. The Werewolves continued the fight within Germany after the surrender, when Germany was occupied. They bombed and destroyed Germany's infrastructure and continued acts of guerilla warfare. In effect, the Werewolves were SS terrorists who were not silenced until several years after the war.

During the course of the war, the Waffen SS proved to be a formidable enemy of the Allied Forces. It was a sophisticated military machine that mass-produced terror. Its members wouldn't think twice about killing a regular German soldier if that soldier showed any lack of courage on the battlefield. The SS lacked the human characteristics of compassion and mercy and possessed the inhuman characteristics of cold-bloodedness and rancor, which effectively made them human savages. To encounter the SS in WWII would compare to happening upon a grizzly bear: to survive, one would have to be calm, maintain one's wits, and expect no mercy.

Cullerton knew of the Malmedy Massacre and had no desire to see those SS bastards during his run to safety. He knew that if he did encounter the SS, he would never see home again. Then he remembered one of the last debriefings at Steeple Morden; they had been told that there were now plain-clothes (civilian-attired) SS who roamed the countryside in Germany. These SS groups killed alleged German deserters on the spot, as well as civilians who were only suspected of cooperating with the British or Americans. He'd learned that the name of this wonderful group of Nazis was der Werwolfe, as named by the infamous Joseph Goebbels himself. *Der Werewolfe. Great name*, Cullerton thought as he smiled ironically and shook his head. *It's incredible*, he thought. *In addition to everything else, I've got to worry about "werewolves" in Germany.* In effect, Cullerton had to avoid everyone, including civilians, on this trek.

Bill rested his head as he leaned back on a great oak tree, in the dark, and exhaled. His breath billowed like cigarette smoke in the cold, dead winter air. It was nearly midnight, and Cullerton realized that he had not eaten in twenty hours, so he opened the first chocolate bar, which tasted good, very good, and gobbled it down quickly. He mustered his mental strength not to eat the other bar; he would save that one for tomorrow. As he leaned back again, his body began to cool down, and he realized that it was very cold. He had lost his leather gloves, and he was ill-prepared for a night outside. Even though it was early spring, it still felt like winter. He pulled brush and leaves around his body for insulation. Cullerton was cold and tired; in order to stay awake and not freeze to death that night he took a Benzedrine tablet.

Cullerton asked himself, *Are there* real *wolves in this forest?* He couldn't remember; as he pondered that thought, he swallowed hard. There were black bears in the wilds of northern Wisconsin, but the wolves were gone there, so there must be bears here, he concluded, and he felt sure there were wolves here as well. The thought of these nocturnal hunters on his trail, along with the Germans, made him very nervous. He checked to make sure he had his sidearm; it was still there. He couldn't continue to sit any longer; he needed to move. Before he got up, Bill listened, and he could have sworn that out there something was looking at him. A chill ran down his spine. He needed to run, now. He verified his heading with his compass and began to move, this time with his right arm in front of his face to block any tree branches.

Cullerton was concerned about crossing paths with any forest or human demons, but he wasn't aware that his greatest enemy was following him, or at least preparing to follow him. Cullerton was on a collision course with destiny. The mountain of sand in the bottom of the hourglass was filling up fast.

In the Black Forest
Day 2 on the Run

At daybreak, Colonel Gruber, his two assassins, and the three devil dogs headed into the forest after Cullerton. The dogs were not yet on a scent, so Gruber's plan was to pursue due west, staggering from the American's start point to pick up his scent along the way. Gruber would move day and night, stopping only for short rest periods. He planned on capturing the American within a day or two, and once he found him, Gruber would then decide how the American would die.

The ill-prepared American flier was Gruber's prey in a sadistic game for which Gruber already knew the outcome. He was an experienced outdoorsman, an accomplished hunter, and it was only a matter of time before the American would be caught by his team. The lone pilot was too far away from the safety of the advancing Allies. The American was doomed.

Ahead in the Black Forest

As the sun came up, Cullerton was still moving. The temperature remained at the freezing point. Bill was exhausted, but he saw a stream up ahead. It was a small stream in a clearing. He stopped and pulled out his cup. He dropped his cup through a thin layer of ice on the top of the slow-moving water. He filled it and dropped in a purification pill. He immediately drained the cup and repeated the process two more times. The water tasted so good; it was very cold and tasted pure. It reminded Bill of the north country back home. If only he could step into the chow line at Steeple Morden, but there would be no food for Cullerton today. He could wait no longer, and he quickly scarfed down the other chocolate bar. He felt that he might be full, but it was a fleeting thought, as the nagging hunger would not cease. He'd been running for thirty-two hours, with only minutes of sleep. Bill needed to stay out of sight and get some sleep.

The sunlight felt good on his face, however, and for the first time in twenty-eight hours he briefly felt warm. But he had to get under cover, so Cullerton found another pine tree and burrowed under it, just as he had the day before, although this time he was alone; this time he could sleep. Within five minutes, the American airman was sound asleep, and it was a deep sleep.

The visions came quickly. Bill was at home with all the people whom he loved. There was laughter.

Bill was flying his Mustang. The pilots were talking on the radio. They were strafing a military convoy. There was a German ambulance back at the hospital, from the front. It would be full of German wounded—pull up, pull up, don't shoot. But passing in the other direction was an ambulance heading toward the front lines. That one should be full of ammunition. It was a target. Bill focused on the ambulance heading toward the front lines and shot it up. It exploded like the ammunition dump that it was—Intel had been correct. His plane flew on, and the dream faded.

Cullerton awoke with a start and struggled to remember where he was. He heard airplanes overhead; the sound of the Merlin engines must have fueled his dream. When he looked into the sky, he saw the Mustangs above. Bill was elated; he realized they were on a mission. It was about 1:30 p.m., Steeple Morden/Cambridge, England time. What time was it in Chicago? What time was it wherever he was? Bill wondered. Cullerton could deny his hunger no longer. He crawled back to the stream and got more water; he also decided to relieve himself here. He did not want any type of creature to track him down by the scent of his urine on the turf. Cullerton looked around and began to head west again.

From within the forest, he could see a farmer's field, so he moved closer to the edge of the forest to get a better look. Cullerton saw women planting potatoes, lots of potatoes, and he noticed that they were under armed guard. They were prisoners, possibly Polish or Russian slave labor, he thought. He kept his eyes on the guards and guessed that because he was closer to Poland, the fair-haired, fair-skinned girls were Polish forced labor.

At sundown, the female field hand prisoners headed off with their armed guards. Watching from a safe distance, Cullerton waited for full darkness before he made his move out to the field. He began to dig in the field with his bare hands. It was cold again, and he dug with his hands for forty-five minutes but could not find one potato. He knew the potatoes had to be there somewhere; he had seen the girls planting them. His hands were raw, and he couldn't dig any longer. Cullerton kicked at the ground out of frustration. Hunger was a continuous existence; he tried to ignore it, but the pangs wouldn't go away. Angry as hell, he kept moving west.

Five Miles Behind

Gruber's team had picked up Bill's scent and was now on the American's trail. They were further behind the American than they had thought. There was no doubt that the American was heading west, but, then again, it didn't take a German rocket scientist to figure out that an American would head west. Gruber had calculated the American's probable foot speed and decided to take a shortcut; the team would intercept the airman tomorrow, around dusk. The Germans moved ahead another mile and set up camp for the night. They had closed the gap on the American; they were positive that they were only four miles behind him, and the Yank was sixty miles from his own lines. Gruber would get him; he was patient and took pleasure in this hunt. As the Germans sat around their fire, Gruber smiled and took a deep drag of his cigarette, as the two SS soldiers watched intently. They saw him smile again; nobody ever saw him smile. The soldiers listened as Gruber speculated on the American they were trailing.

The colonel, in his elitist SS manner, guessed that the American, who appeared to be an accomplished pilot, would be an intelligent athlete of some sort, and probably from a well-to-do family. The two sergeants nodded and asked what else the colonel suspected of the American.

Gruber continued. He anticipated that the American wouldn't use deception or trickery in his efforts to get to the American lines; rather, he would head on a predictable, straight course to save time, since he was desperate to get back to the safety of his own lines. Gruber believed that at some point the American would get too hungry and cold and would perhaps try to surrender to a civilian because it was near the end of the war. To Gruber, it was very unlikely that the American was any kind of real outdoorsman, but rather a typical American party boy type who had become a flier to impress the girls. The sergeants nodded in agreement; based on what they had heard about Americans and seen in American movies, it seemed logical. Gruber also added that he anticipated getting the American before he gave up, because he wanted to kill him. The two sergeants nodded again, without saying a word, because they, too, would be glad to kill the American pilot, with or without Gruber.

It would be to Gruber's dismay to learn that Bill was an accomplished outdoorsman from his many summers living and working outdoors in the Northwoods of Wisconsin and the Upper Peninsula of Michigan. During those summers, Cullerton had worked at Bill Jameson's fishing and hunting lodge, which was owned by Bill's grandfather. He was an experienced hunter and felt at home outdoors. Although he had partied like a playboy for six months after high-school graduation, he wasn't really a playboy, because it was only seven months after high school when Cullerton had joined the Army. Up until this point, the larger part of Cullerton's adult life had been spent in the Army.

Gruber, however, was enjoying the hunt and would enjoy the kill, as well. Getting there really was half of the fun, and it wouldn't be long. He nudged one of the hounds and tossed it a piece of his raw meat.

Five Miles Ahead

Cullerton knew he had to make speed tonight. Banging into trees and looking for potatoes last night had cost him time and the distance that he needed. He stayed close to the edge of the forest this night to make up for last night. There was partial moonlight, and while he had spent most of his time sitting in a pilot's seat during his time in the war, Cullerton was now moving, on foot, through a forest, stopping only to check his compass. Moving rapidly, Bill ducked low to avoid the hanging branches, sidestepped rotting stumps, and juked around protruding roots.

He had moved a couple of miles when he spotted a bridge over a flowing creek. The fates began to intervene. He looked around, but there was no one. He had a bad feeling about crossing the bridge out in the open under bright moonlight, so instead, he moved upstream to jump the creek. He calculated the distance across and made a running leap, only to fall backward right into the creek. "Goddamn it," he cursed. As he got out of the water and pulled himself up to the shoreline, he saw two armed soldiers step out of the forest.

"*Sprechen Sie Deutsch?*" one asked.

Cullerton shook his head and said, "No."

"*Sind Sie Amerikaner?*" Cullerton nodded yes.

With their guns pointed at him, the guards motioned for him to raise his hands.

"*Rouse, rouse!*"

He stood there, hands up, as the guards searched him. They took his gun and his knife and rifle-butted Cullerton in the gut. Bill doubled over and the guard kneed him in the midsection, knocking him down and leaving him gasping for air. The older guard spoke to the young one, but Cullerton couldn't hear what he said; he was trying to recover. The young guard then kicked Cullerton in the side, twice, for good measure.

The guards stepped back as the younger one yelled, *"Rouse, rouse!"* Cullerton staggered to his feet as his anger mounted. When he stood upright, he looked the guard in the eye; they stared at each other. For the first time in the war, Bill knew he could kill this sadistic punk if he had only had his gun, and by the look in the guard's eyes, Cullerton knew that he felt the same way.

Bill saw the official Hitler Youth knife the guard had on him. The older guard saw his partner aim his rifle at Bill; he was going to shoot. The other guard yelled at him and motioned for Cullerton to move. They all headed into the woods.

Cullerton thought that this was it, that they were going to bring him into the woods and shoot him, but after walking for about thirty minutes straight north, they came upon a cabin. Bill was somewhat surprised that they hadn't killed him yet. Bill realized that the old-timer had saved his life, for now.

The two guards took Cullerton to a small cabin in the forest, where it was warm and dry. They set his gun, knife, and supplies on a table and tied him to a chair near the fire in the hearth. The young guard butted Cullerton in the ribs with his rifle once again. The older guard had to stop him from doing it a second time. Both guards were now heatedly discussing something; Cullerton didn't understand what they were saying to each other, although he had a pretty good idea.

It was still the middle of the night as the two soldiers' heated discussion continued. After their discussion, the young soldier left the cabin rather angrily. Through a window, Cullerton saw his direction. The young soldier went south, back toward the river. Cullerton was surprised by this, but he figured that the guard was headed to alert someone, perhaps regular Army, to take Cullerton off their hands. The older soldier had apparently won the argument or discussion, because he sat back in a chair and closed his eyes.

Bill turned toward the older soldier, who didn't seem worried that Cullerton would try to escape. Cullerton's adrenalin was pumping, but he didn't try to talk to the soldier or make any move to draw attention to himself. Bill just sat still beside the crackling fire watching the soldier nod off. Within a half hour, the solider had drifted into a sound sleep. Cullerton had been working on freeing himself from his rope bonds, and he was close to getting free. He knew he had to make a move soon, because the other guard would return with reinforcements, or real soldiers, or worse.

Cullerton quietly shook his ropes loose and jumped the sleeping guard as he grabbed his .45 pistol off the table. Cullerton had no intention of shooting the older guard, as the old man was helpless at the time. Instead, Cullerton tied the soldier's hands behind his back, talking to the German in agitated English. He grabbed his survival kit from the table, holstered his pistol, and snatched a loaf of bread from the table, along with his knife. Cullerton decided to change his original direction; any trailing Germans wouldn't expect Cullerton to double back and head south, so that's exactly what he did. As he left, he looked at the old soldier and nodded, and the old soldier nodded back. Cullerton headed back on course, due west and well south of his original path.

Cullerton's brief capture by the Home Guard had bought him time, because Colonel Gruber would not intercept him where he expected the American to be. Cullerton ran as fast and as carefully as he could in the dark, to make up for lost time.

It was another crisp, clear moonlit night, and four hours after dark, Cullerton moved in the trees for cover and came upon another creek. The creek that was cutting across his path was too wide to ford. Bill was getting nervous about crossing this creek; he needed to find a bridge, so he moved along the banks. After heading south he spotted an old stone bridge that appeared to be unguarded. Cullerton watched and waited a few minutes; it looked deserted, so Bill walked from the woods out into the open toward the bridge, acting as if he were a German citizen, hands in pockets and began to cross. However, Bill hadn't seen the guard who was sitting on the floor of the bridge, resting behind the protective stone wall.

As Cullerton approached, the startled guard, dressed in a regular German Army issue uniform, stood up. Bill didn't break stride as he walked with his hands in his pockets.

"Guten Abend," Bill said as he approached, in an attempt to walk by the guard.

"Halt!" the German said sternly. Cullerton said nothing and kept walking over the bridge. He didn't want any trouble.

"Der Namen!" the guard yelled. *"Papieren,"* he yelled.

The bridge guard, who was taller and older than the American, stepped in front of Cullerton, brought his rifle around and aimed at him. Cullerton brought his knife out with the intention of killing the guard. He stepped into the guard before the guard could get his rifle under control, and he stabbed him. Cullerton looked into the man's eyes as he drove the knife with adrenalin force through the uniform and up into his chest.

The soldier exhaled and collapsed into Bill's arms. Cullerton was consumed by a feeling of regret. He hadn't wanted this. He wished the guy had just let him pass. As the soldier collapsed, Cullerton moved him to the edge of the bridge and gently slipped him into the water. He dropped the man's helmet and gun into the water after him, leaving no trace of the guard. The flowing water quietly whisked the soldier's body down the stream. Cullerton was sick to his stomach over the encounter, though he hadn't had a choice. He would rather have killed that sadistic Hitler youth earlier that night than this soldier. Cullerton quickly made the sign of the cross, asked for forgiveness, and went over the bridge. Once he got into the woods, he was able to move faster with the guidance of the full moon. Bill would never forget the face of the soldier on the bridge.

It was two hours before sunrise, and Bill needed to rest. It was another cold night, well below freezing. Bill took a Benzedrine pill to ensure a light sleep. He wondered how he could sleep anyway, since he was so hungry.

April 10
Day 3 on the Run

Cullerton awoke before dawn amidst the naked branches and detritus of the forest. He was shivering and shaking from the winterlike cold. His pants were frozen stiff, and his feet were numb. He pulled tighter into a fetal position. He lay on his side and attempted to open his eyes, but they wouldn't open. The moisture from his eyes had frozen his eyelids shut. He pulled his hands out from the relative warmth of his armpits to break the ice from his lashes. He had to move and get his blood back into circulation. Bill looked up and saw that it was cloudy. Day three in the Black Forest was under way. Cullerton pressed on for hours during the day, but by afternoon he was exhausted again. Without the sun, the temperature had warmed up only a little, and Cullerton needed to rest. Worn out and starved, he decided to lie down for a while.

South of Cullerton

On their trek, Colonel Gruber looked at his watch. It was noon and these were his woods. He estimated that the American would have to sleep at least two hours and slow down to forage for food. Gruber's hounds and two snipers would catch him later today.

The German group arrived at their intercept point and waited several hours for the American, but their prey did not show. Gruber was furious; perhaps this American would be a challenge after all. Maybe the flier was cleverer than he had thought. Gruber couldn't have guessed that the American had been caught and delayed by the Home Guard the night before. Gruber sent one of his sergeants back along their track to see if he could determine anything. The SS colonel would have to rethink his strategy.

Three miles to the north and two miles west of the Germans, Cullerton slept fitfully, and he awoke in the late afternoon. As he awoke from a frozen sleep, Bill stumbled about the forest like a drunken sailor. His muscles did not respond well, and his head ached. It wasn't just the cold; he was weak from starvation. He was lightheaded and dizzy, and he knew that he needed to eat something, anything. He stopped, at no place in particular, got on his knees, and clawed at the earth. Since it was still winter, the ground had yet to fully thaw, therefore, digging for worms, or night crawlers, was out of the question. Bill wasn't thinking clearly. He grabbed a rock and clenched it in his left hand. He was going to kill the first live thing he saw.

Bill thought to himself, "If I hit a bird, rabbit, squirrel, or whatever the hell it's going to be, it'll be by the grace of God." Bill knew full well that it'd be hard enough to strike a swift little animal with a rock if he were healthy and well, let alone hungry and weary.

He could barely keep his eyes open as he wobbled through the forest, occasionally stopping to lean up against a tree. Out of his left ear, he could hear a light rustle in the brush. It startled him for a brief moment, and then he zeroed in on a small rabbit that sat about twelve feet from him. He stood quietly to gather every ounce of stealth and coordination he could, to kill his prey. The rabbit was not simply flesh and blood, but rather it was a power cell, a battery that could give Bill another day or two of life. He took a deep breath, and as he wound up to pitch the rock, he lost control and let out a loud grunt. As he released the rock, he couldn't regain control of his body and his forward momentum sent him to the ground, rolling and landing on his back. He passed out when he hit the ground. The rabbit was out of sight before Bill even released the rock.

As he lay, seemingly out cold, images passed in and out of his mind, dreams. As he lay there looking upward, Bill saw several large ravens circling the skies of a setting sun. He knew the black birds were hovering over him. He closed his eyes, and when he opened them again, he was still lying on the forest floor, this time looking to the east. The sun had set, and the moon was shining through the trees. He looked to the forest horizon and behind the leafless trees was a menacing purple sky. Against this sky there appeared the silhouettes of a platoon of nine Waffen SS soldiers slowly breaking the horizon as they walked in Bill's direction. They were wearing long black trench coats and their faces were in shadow. They were getting closer to Bill with every pound of his beating heart. As he reached for his gun, the image faded, and Bill sank deeper into sleep.

Another dream emerged in his mind. This time he could see himself lying on the forest floor, dead, while three crows lingered over his body. One, on his right side near his stomach, was tearing through his shirt. The other two crows were surrounded his face, one picking at his eyeball while the other began pulling and tearing at his tongue. More crows emerged and fought for Bill's remains. They began to squawk. He awoke in a frenzy and began to feel for his eyes. As soon as he realized it was only in his mind did he notice that the squawking had not ceased. He looked up and saw a large raven staring and yelling at him from a tree only fifteen feet away.

Bill's dreams collectively served as a dark premonition. He knew if he did not eat now, he would die where he lay. The only question was how he would die. Using his pistol was his only option to get the bird. He wondered whether the Germans would hear him. Most likely, he thought. He looked at his pistol in his left hand; Bill knew this was the only way if he were going to have any chance of survival. He had to risk the noise of a gunshot. With a rather large bird within his grasp, the time was now. He cocked, raised, aimed, and fired his pistol at the bird's head.

A perfect shot. The bird's head exploded as the gunshot echoed through the forest. The black feathery body fell to the ground. Bill ran over and hastily grabbed the crow in his left hand and took the bird to his mouth. He grasped it so that the open neck served as a spigot and he squeezed the corpse as though it were a piece of fruit yielding the sweetest and most delicious juice ever tasted by man. To Bill, this was not mere satiation, but life. He felt as though every drop of blood was another mile he could run. He began to suck the neck for every last drop of blood until it began to slow. When the body of the crow appeared dry, Bill ripped off most of the feathers and bit into the scantily meated bones until there wasn't anything left. Sometimes crunching a warm bone, he would suck on it before he spit out. When he finished consuming the bird, Bill laid back on the forest floor. His mouth, chin, and neck were stained with blood. The raven tasted terrible, but that was of no concern to Bill. After a while, he started to focus, and he stretched his body as the proteins from his crow dinner almost instantaneously gave him new life.

Getting to a safe haven was not about seeing family and friends again, nor was it about flying nor getting out of this hell-on-earth war-ravaged country. His goal now was about surviving. The only thing Bill needed to do to defeat his enemies was reach the safety of the Allied lines. He thought about the noise of the gunshot and realized that he needed to move out of the area. He quickly got up and began to move westward, further into the forest.

In the Distance

In the early evening, the two German soldiers and three hounds heard a single shot in the distance. It was a pistol shot, but not a German pistol. The three dogs pivoted in that direction, northwest of their current position. The American had made his mistake, and in Gruber's mind, it was a fatal error. They expected the American to be on the move so the hunters headed northwest. They had a bead on the American, and they would get him tomorrow for sure. They would begin to travel early the next day, locate the American, and move in after nightfall.

Ahead in the Woods

The sun had set and the forest was beginning to become cold and damp. Bill had been moving for hours and decided it was time to rest, so he sat up against a tree, gathered up surrounding brush for insulation, and swallowed a Benzedrine pill to avoid sleep.

In spite of the pill he had taken, Bill was startled awake only minutes later by a loud rustling noise moving toward him. He couldn't see anything, but he could hear the crackling of branches. Bill grabbed his pistol and pointed it into the darkness. The noise then stopped and Bill remained quiet. He heard someone say, "Hello."

"Who's there, goddamn it!" Bill yelled.

"Do not fear me; I can help you. First, put your weapon away. I will not hurt you," replied a man in German-accented English.

"Why should I trust a German? I could shoot you dead and be no worse for the wear."

"I know what hunts you. I know where it is. And I know when it will meet you."

"Show your face!" Cullerton demanded.

A German civilian walked into view, lit a match, put it up to his face, and said, "I am Helmut Bauer. If you want to get back to your army, you will trust me and follow." He then lit a cigarette with the match, which brightly lit his face, and motioned to Bill, offering him a cigarette. Bill approached and nodded yes. Bauer lit Cullerton's cigarette from his own and handed it to Bill. The German was over six feet in height and looked to be in his early forties, in good physical

116

condition, with a weathered face. He eyes were menacing, dark brown, not the so-called Aryan blue eyes that Cullerton expected. "Why isn't this guy in the German Army?" Cullerton wondered. Then Bill remembered the plain clothes SS, German "Werewolves." Bill grew more suspicious. This did not feel right.

"Why would you want to help an American?"

"What is your name, American?"

"Bill."

"American Bill, do you think the German people aren't victims as well? Do you think everyone here believes in the Fuhrer?"

"A downed pilot, who was a friend of mine, was killed by German villagers. Not exactly a hero's welcome. So, yes, I do think everyone here believes in that son of a bitch Hitler."

"Not this German, and there are many more . . . believe me. So, will you join me?"

Bill thought to himself, *He must be alone. If there were others with him, I would be dead now. What is this guy's game?*

"Join you for what?" Bill asked.

"I will take you to the American army. They are forty kilometers north-northeast."

Bill was cautious but still listening to the German. Helmut came off as sincere, yet strange, and Bill wanted to believe him. "Are you armed?" Bill asked.

"Of course, I have the best pistol in the world," Bauer replied.

"What? Did you rob a dead American soldier?"

Bauer laughed. "No. A dead Waffen SS. You don't really believe that an American Colt is better than a German Luger, do you?"

"Fuck you," Bill replied, harshly.

"I do have a magazine for a Colt, if you want it."

"Absolutely."

Bauer pulled a full Colt .45 magazine from his satchel and handed it to Bill. Bill looked at it and said, "So you *did* rob an American for this?"

"No, American Bill, the same Waffen SS body."

Bill was silenced. He did not have total confidence in Bauer.

"Now, American Bill, we must be silent. There are evil eyes and ears all over this forest. If we are to get to your army, we must slip through the German lines without notice." Bill nodded and looked around.

The unlikely duo walked for a while, and Bill lagged with exhaustion. Bauer, though edgy, realized Bill needed to stop and rest. They came to a pine tree under which they could both lie.

"Rest here, American Bill. I am going to check the area; I'll be gone only a couple of minutes," Bauer said. Bill practically fell to the ground and rolled under the sweeping pines, pulled his body into the fetal position, and fell asleep immediately.

A short time later, Bill awoke, looked around under the tree, and found only Bauer's satchel. Bill heard loud breathing beyond the pine branches. He sat up and his heart began to race. He could see beyond the tree by parting some branches. When Bill looked out, the moon shone bright down to the forest floor. Though he couldn't see anyone, Bill assumed it was Bauer, which wasn't comforting enough. Suddenly, Bill heard a figure start to run. It was running in circles around the tree, and it was breathing heavily.

Bill pulled out his pistol and checked for his new magazine. The running continued, as if to toy with him. Finally the running ceased; he looked out again and saw someone standing in the moonlight. Bill stepped out of the branches and said, "Move and I'll shoot you dead!" The man didn't respond; he was taking deep, fast breaths. "Bauer?" he asked. Bill stepped closer. The man's breathing turned to a near snarl. Between the moon shadows of the leafless trees, he thought he saw a wolf. "What the hell?" Bill said as it approached, now only six feet away from the man. He thought, *If it's Bauer, I don't want to shoot him, though I am not sure.* So he quickly pistol whipped the man in the back of the head. The man barely budged, and Bill was stunned. He turned around and backhanded Bill, which sent him flying backward. After Bill landed, he looked up and didn't see anything; the man was out of sight. Bill heard a howl, one that he had heard before, on a fishing trip in Canada. It was the unmistakable howl of a wolf, and it was close, nearly thirty feet away, somewhere in the darkness nearby. "Holy shit!" Bill yelled.

Bill thought he was hallucinating. It was a beast, a fanged creature, larger than a wolf but smaller than a buffalo. The beast leapt from the wood and jumped on Bill, pinning him to the ground. The creature snarled at Cullerton, drooling on his face. *This is a nightmare,* he thought, as he stared back at the glowing red eyes. In its pupils Bill could see swastikas. It appeared the creature might leave, but then it pulled its head back and snapped it down, latching directly onto Bill's throat and tearing it open. Bill yelled; he grabbed his neck and sat straight up. "Fucking werewolves," he said under his breath, his heart pounding. "Goddamn it!" There was no Bauer; there never had been.

Bill stood up, now fully alert after such a startling nightmare, and he began to move on. With his first step, he tripped and fell on top of what he automatically assumed was a wolf. Bill's pulse jumped again. The animal made a couple of attempts to bite Bill, and it also kicked at him. Bill realized that this was only a deer nesting for the night. Both Bill and the deer had nearly died of fright. Bill moved on, if somewhat cautiously.

April 11
Day 4 on the Run

Cullerton moved slowly during the day, trying not to be seen, and he looked for food all the while. He couldn't help but reflect on the crows and werewolves that had haunted him the night before. It gave him the creeps. He found himself looking over his shoulder from time to time, making sure that no one was following him. Early in the afternoon, Bill came up to a small village that was unavoidable. As he passed through the bushes that came up to a narrow gravel pathway, he spotted a wheelbarrow that was turned over on its side. He grabbed the wheelbarrow, put his hat away, and began whistling as he pushed it down the main street of the village. He would nod at the German townsfolk and softly mutter *"Guten Morgen"* as he passed them by. The people nodded back and were unfazed by his presence; he was incognito. He passed a small shop which smelled of food and home cooking. His head began to ache and his stomach twisted as he passed by. Finally, reaching the other side of town, Bill saw the woods; he looked around and swallowed hard before he ditched the wheelbarrow and crept back into the forest. He glanced at his compass and headed west by south to avoid a labor farm he saw in the distance. He was starting to talk to himself now.

It was a dark night, darker than usual and it was cold again. Cullerton had rested deep in the forest and he was as cold as hell was hot. Awakened by the cold, he heard that same alarming sound; it was the deep wail of a hound, and by the bellow of its voice he knew that it was a large wolflike hound. It was the sound of a hound on a trail, and it was getting closer. Bill slapped himself, thinking that he was sleeping again, but he was awake, and the hound was coming for him. Bill Cullerton, who had better than perfect eyesight, looked deep into the woods as he grabbed his .45 and his knife. He could see nothing. He had to act quickly, because the monster was very close now. Bill could hear it moving through the forest toward him. Yes, it sounded like only one creature, and Cullerton's pulse jumped when the creature howled again. He looked to his left and saw a large tree, probably an oak, about ten feet away. Bill ran to the tree and knelt down low with his back to it. He knelt on his right knee, propped his left elbow on the left knee, grasped his gun with his left hand and steadied it with his right. His hunter instincts took over as he focused on the direction of the sound. He heard the hound coming through the brush over the forest floor. His heart pounded. It growled, deep and menacing, still concealed in the darkness. *Where is it?* he wondered as he heard it coming closer and finally into sight. He had never seen a hound like this before; it was some kind of *uberhund*, a German superhound. The monster was bounding toward him from fifteen feet away. Cullerton didn't panic as the monster leapt at him. "Now!" he shouted and fired once and dove to the side. The hound slammed into the tree where Bill had knelt. It was stone dead. Cullerton stared at it in disbelief as his heart continued to pound. He had never seen a dog that looked as powerful and menacing; it could have torn him apart. Instinctively, upon realizing what his fate could have been, Cullerton aimed his pistol into the darkness and fired twice more, one shot slightly to the left of the direction from which the dead monster had come and one shot slightly to the right of it. The two rounds went quickly, deeply, and harmlessly into the darkness. They were wasted shots, which bought Cullerton only a minute feeling of safety. He glanced at the dead creature and then listened to the forest. There was no sound at all. He knew danger was nearby. He checked his compass and bolted. Propelled by adrenaline and fear, Bill ran in the opposite direction. He ran for nearly an hour, stumbling and falling over objects. As he became tired and delirious, staggering from tree to tree, he heard howling in the distance. There was another animal out there, but it was still far off.

Colonel Gruber and the others approached the dead hound. The remaining two hounds howled and paced. Gruber looked at the wound in the dead animal. The shot was in the center of the dog's chest. Gruber now knew for certain that the American was armed and did not intend to surrender. Gruber reasoned that the American had probably been a hunter in the past, since he'd remained cool under pressure. The Germans intended to camp there that night, bury his beloved dog, and plan the attack for the following night.

April 12
Day 5 on the Run

Back home, President Roosevelt died. Americans mourned, while most of the Germans celebrated. Bill had no way of knowing about the president; in fact, he didn't even know what day it was.

Cullerton kept moving all day. He had heard the howling, which sounded to be at least two more hounds. Cullerton had only four shots left. *Distance.* He needed to come up with a plan to put distance between himself and them.

"Sleep for an hour," he said to himself. But he didn't. He moved on.

"That must have been a farmer's dog on the loose, a family watchdog," he tried to convince himself. But Cullerton knew better. Bill had gotten a good look at the creature; it was a Nazi animal. Bill wished he had back those two extra shots he'd fired. *I'm safe now for the moment,* he thought. *Rest, rest . . .*

Cullerton moved deeper into the dark woods and lay down against the largest tree he could find. It was evening now. He yearned to be back in Steeple Morden in his bed, out of the elements, warm and fed. He hadn't had any real food, except the raw crow, in five and a half days. *Oh, to feel the warmth of a bed*, he thought. It was close to 9:00 p.m., and he would sleep for only an hour, he told himself, before he moved on. Surely his fears would override his exhaustion and he wouldn't oversleep.

Cullerton was awakened by a sharp *crack* not too far away, perhaps a quarter mile. It was pitch-black out, with no wind, and it was very cold. He was freezing again. He glanced at his watch; it was 4:00 a.m. Although his feet, hands, and nose were frozen, he was alert, and the adrenaline was again coursing through his system. "Hell hound, dark, in the woods" . . . and again he heard the blood-curdling, shudder-inducing, bellowing howl. It was one of the other Nazi monsters, and it was on Cullerton's scent. After all this time they were still on him. Cullerton had traded distance for sleep, and now Gruber and his hunting party were about to get him. The realization came to Bill that he had been hunted from the moment he left the wreck of the *Miss Steve*. Cullerton listened intently. He heard only one howl. *What happened to the second hound?* he wondered. *Why send one at a time?*

Cullerton was in as good a defensive position as he could be at this new large tree. He would take the offensive from here. Judging by the direction of the howl, the monster would clear the brush over there and only be visible to him for about fifteen feet in the small clearing. Cullerton would have about ninety seconds to kill the hound before it got to him. This would take strategic planning.

On the Trail Behind

This had been a longer chase than Gruber had expected, and he was exhausted, as were his men. But the two remaining hounds were difficult to restrain, as they tugged and pulled at their leashes in the excitement of the search. As the SS team moved in on Cullerton, about one quarter of a mile away from where Bill was waiting, Gruber stepped on a rotten branch that lay across a slight depression on the ground. The cracking noise of the branch resonated like a cannon. The Germans were compromised. The two snipers traded glances with slight eye rolls. They had lost the element of surprise.

Gruber was furious with himself. He knew the American had heard it. He unmuzzled one of the hounds, and it immediately bawled the horrible wail of a hound on the scent. Gruber smiled now because he knew the American had to be intimidated; this would send a chill up his spine. The American bastard pilot and killer of Germans would die a horrible death this night, and Gruber wanted the American to know it.

Gruber was no fool. He was an experienced and well-trained Waffen SS colonel. His own personal Waffen Hund Gruppe had trained these blended-breed hounds that were going to do the job and tear the American apart for him.

Gruber had learned his lesson after last night's encounter with the American, so he shifted strategy. He knew the American might be low on ammunition, that he was formidable and armed, tired and starving. Now that he had the American's attention, he released his second hound, and as this one let out his powerful howl, Gruber released the third hound, Rolf, who didn't make a sound. Rolf was the largest of the pack of hellhounds, and the stealthiest of them all.

The second hound was on the scent, while Rolf was off and angling to the left, behind the second hound, heading in the same general direction, although very stealthily.

Earlier that evening, when Cullerton sat down to rest, he had devised a plan. He decided to use an old American Indian trick of setting a false trail. To start, Cullerton picked a large tree, fifteen feet away from the brush line and situated in a small clearing. He would use this tree as protection to back up against. To set the false path, he crossed perpendicular at the brush line, both left and right of the tree where he would wait. He set a trail about twenty feet long each way by spitting and urinating in a straight line. The false trail was, in fact, a scent shield set at the edge of the clearing, divided two ways, allowing Cullerton time to aim and shoot while the dog had to decide which direction to follow. So he sat down at his tree and faced the direction from which he had originally come. As Cullerton waited, he started to second-guess his plan. He was thinking that maybe he would need one of those bullets for himself.

Adrenaline was coursing through Bill's veins. He waited near a tree with his .45 at the ready. "Bring on the monster. Let's go. Let's get it over with, you son of a bitch!" he hollered into the darkness. Seconds later, the hound bellowed back his fearsome howl.

The lead hound fleet-footed toward Cullerton; the sound of his approach was not as rollicking as the hound the night before. Cullerton remained attentive; he knew what to listen for. The hound was on Cullerton's path in the woods, and unbeknownst to Bill, parallel to the lead hound and just behind it, Rolf was moving in.

Cullerton tarried at the edge of the brush line; the lead hound ignored the false trail to the right and the trail straight ahead. The hound hesitated and turned to take the trail to his left; it worked, he took part of the bait. When the hound turned left, it gave Cullerton time to aim. He aimed, fired, and missed. Without changing suit, the hound turned and lunged at Cullerton, staring him directly in the eye. Cullerton fired again and rolled as the hound leapt at him with great alacrity. The hound whimpered from the blow to his stomach and collapsed dead to the ground. As Cullerton rose up on his right knee, the other hound leapt at him from his right side. Cullerton was caught off guard and aghast by the emergence of a third creature. As Bill turned, he could see that the unexpected hound was coming at his throat. It was larger than the others and viscerally terrifying. The only thing Bill could do was to nose-dive toward the monster in midair. Cullerton dove to the ground and half rolled onto his back. The hound hit the ground beyond Cullerton and turned to grab Cullerton by his throat. As it lunged at him, Bill fired once more. The hound fell, exhaling on the way down. The hound's ugly head collapsed on Cullerton's chest; their hearts pounded into one another as they laid against the base of a large oak tree, a tree which bore silent witness to the strange encounter that had just occurred. Cullerton recovered; his survival instincts were sharp.

Are there anymore? he wondered, and took a look around. His adrenaline surged again. He jumped up and took a last confirming look at the two dead monsters. He took advantage of his adrenaline rush and ran. With one bullet left, he ran like hell. He *was* in hell. He had been in the Black Forest for five days. Where was he running to?

Colonel Gruber was incensed. His three finest hounds had been killed by the American flyer. Gruber would not sleep again until he searched out the man who had killed his beloved hounds. He dismissed his sniper assassins and sent them back to Ansbach. It was one-on-one now, just him and the American, the way it should have been from the start. No more strategies, no more games; he would kill the American himself, tomorrow. He would not stop searching until the American was dead. Colonel Gruber buried his two dead hounds, and while Waffen SS soldiers don't cry, Gruber's eyes glazed over as he dug out the graves. Hatred filled his icy-cold blue eyes.

For You the War Is Over

April 13 (Friday)
Day 6 on the Run

On his adrenaline-surging quest to survive, Cullerton had moved as far as he could during the night. It was daybreak now on Friday morning. He did the math in his head and chuckled at the irony of the day; it was Friday the thirteenth. He had already evaded the Germans, except for his brief capture, for five full days. He had killed one German soldier, three German attack dogs, one crow, and had "captured" one German soldier. He knew there was still plenty of danger, but he was trying to be positive about the situation. He was optimistic and had the will to survive. He figured he must be closer to the Allied lines at this point, especially if the Americans were pushing east. He might only be ten or twelve miles from safety, nonetheless, a discouraging distance.

Meanwhile, his hunger pangs brought up memories of the crow from a few days back, and he decided that he'd save his last bullet for something special. He exhaled in mock humor, talking to himself again. *Starting my sixth day in the forest, one bullet left, no food, and freezing, but at least I'm losing some weight.* With that he got up and began his trek west. Bill had to be positive. The alternative was to give up. If he gave up mentally, he would be dead physically. He had to keep moving. As he walked, he realized his pants were riding lower on his hips. He pulled them up and tightened his belt two notches. Starvation and a lot of running would do that.

Bill spotted another farmer's field being tended by female prisoners. They were planting potatoes again, as far as Bill could tell. He crept closer to the edge of the forest. The overwhelming sense of hunger was urging him to take chances that he wouldn't normally take. He got as close as he could get to one of the girls, so close that he could see her face. She was a teenager, around seventeen years old, only a few years younger than Bill. The girl had many potatoes in her basket. Cullerton looked around and didn't see a single guard in any direction. *Am I overlooking the guards because I'm so damn hungry?* he wondered.

Bill looked around again and then bolted from the bush and approached her. She was startled and almost screamed. Luckily, she didn't. Bill got close to her face, gently placed his index finger over his lips, looked her square in the eye, and said, *"Amerikaner, Americanski,"* while pointing to himself. She did not scream. She nodded in silence. Cullerton motioned to his mouth and pointed to her potatoes. She gave him three for his pockets, and he started eating the fourth while he stood there. He held a fifth potato. He ate the potato, covered in dirt, as he looked at the girl. She simply watched him and did not speak.

"Danke. Thank you," he uttered in English, mouth full.

She nodded in acknowledgment, with a pensive look. She pointed to herself and said *"Polski."*

Bill responded, "You are Polish? *Polski?"* She nodded and smiled at him.

He tried to communicate with her. *"Sprechen Sie Deutsch?"* She shook her head no, and pinched her fingers together indicating that perhaps she spoke a little German. "Where are you from in Poland?" he asked.

"Polski, ja," she said. He smiled at her. Bill realized that he couldn't speak her language and she couldn't speak his and that jabbering in the potato field could get him shot. She looked at Bill and didn't speak but motioned for him to take her with him. Bill stopped chewing and swallowed hard. There was no mistaking that sign language. He looked at her and then at the forest.

Cullerton's brain was starting to grasp the rather large dilemma he was in at the moment, as he stood in an open potato field, an easy target for any half-blind German soldier. What was he to do? He continued to assess the situation.

If I take her, she'll slow me down. And since I've already been caught twice, it would be very risky. The Germans may still be following me. That would not be good for either of us. Yet, here she is a prisoner. She is from somewhere else, as I am. She has given me this food and she hasn't given me up. Oh God . . . would she scream if I said no? Maybe I should take her. The thoughts clashed in his head.

More thoughts crowded his head as he stared at her. *No. She is safer here. The war is almost over, and she'll be liberated, if they don't kill her first. If I take her, I might get us both killed. There's no way around this. I can't take her. She has to stay. But if I tell her this, will she give me up?*

His thoughts continued to race. He hated to have to tell her she couldn't come with him. Cullerton was in another tough spot. He tried to speak to her in English: "I don't have much choice. Two of us together won't make it. I can't take you. You are safer here." She looked into his eyes as he spoke, gently but urgently, to her. She didn't understand a word he said.

The decision was clear. He could not take her along with him. He touched her on the shoulder in a gesture of reassurance, while shaking his head no and all the while thanking her for the food.

"Danke, danke for potato . . . No, *nein.* No, you cannot go. You must stay . . ."

"*Auf wiedersehen*, pretty girl. *Auf wiedersehen.*"

She stared at him as he started to step away, and then he put up his hand to wave goodbye. He turned and headed to the bush. When he got there he turned back toward the girl. She hadn't moved. She was still standing there staring at him, but at last, slowly, she waved back to him. He knew then that she would not give him up. He nodded to her in thanks and then turned back into the forest.

Cullerton kept moving west. His encounter with the girl was a godsend for more reasons than just the nourishment from the potatoes. He had talked with someone, and even better, she had not tried to kill him, in fact, she had smiled at him. It didn't hurt that she was a young and pretty girl. He was more alert as a result of the food and the encounter. He wondered if she had thought the same thing. How long had it been since someone had smiled at her? He ate the other potatoes as he moved along. *Maybe I should have gotten another potato*, he thought. For the first time in nearly six days he wasn't hungry.

It was getting late in the afternoon. Shadows were growing and beginning to obscure the profiles of the trees in the forest. Everything was starting to blur together before his eyes. Then it began.

Artillery began to pepper the forest around him. Cullerton knew that being in a forest unprotected was more dangerous than being in the open during an artillery attack. When the explosive shells hit high in the trees, a person was at a threefold risk: first, the shrapnel from the exploding rounds could expand in all directions; second, the force of the exploding tree sent shards of wood under extreme velocity in all directions. Impalement had killed many soldiers. Third, falling branches from the damaged trees could kill you as well. Cullerton knew this and he knew he had to get out of the area as fast as he could. He knew by the direction and the sound of the incoming rounds that this was American artillery. His own guys were inadvertently shelling him. His back was against another large oak.

He looked around from the tree to a small clearing that looked to lead in the direction to safety. He stepped away from the tree and ran.

Cullerton had sprinted no more than ten steps from the tree, dodging branches, when he collided with a soldier who was running in the other direction. They crashed into each other and fell, and they stared at each other. Neither soldier had expected to see the other. Both jumped up, and when his vision focused, Cullerton saw that he had run into about six retreating Germans. They were as startled as he was; they too were seeking safety from the American artillery barrage. The shells continued to explode nearby and above; the seven men all stared at each other. Six of them were staring at Cullerton.

The Germans swung their rifles to the ready. Cullerton had his hand on his .45, but he did not draw. This was almost a Mexican standoff. Cullerton saw the lapel insignia on the German officer and the insignias on the helmets of two of the other soldiers who were ready to shoot him.

Captain Bill Cullerton, who had successfully avoided starvation and evaded permanent capture, as well as death by man and beast, and had been on the run over the last five days, was once again staring death in the face. Only three of these soldiers were in the regular German Army and the other three were the dreaded Waffen SS German troops retreating. The SS on the black lapels and a silver skull on the officer's cap indicated that this was a deadly situation; in fact, it was worse than the three hellhounds. Cullerton gulped, without moving his head. He cast his eyes around for an escape—no exit. His hand was still on the .45. Perhaps this was a great picture, but it was a hopeless situation, and Cullerton knew it.

Colonel Gruber approached from the left of Cullerton, gesturing for Cullerton to release his grip on his weapon, and he did. The other soldiers watched curiously. Colonel Gruber stood with aplomb;

Cullerton looked him in the eye. Neither of the men flinched. Gruber took Cullerton's sidearm and motioned for him to stay put. The officer walked over to his men and they discussed the situation. As Cullerton listened to them mutter their plans in German, he watched their body language, but could make nothing of it. While he stood there, thoughts ran through his mind. *Should I run? No, they'll shoot me on the spot. I should stay put,* he told himself as he held back the urge to bolt. *Are they talking about taking me prisoner?* he wondered. *Unlikely,* he decided. *Given the history of the SS, they won't, but there are three regular Army soldiers; maybe they will prevail.* Cullerton's heart pounded as he continued to look for opportunities to escape. He didn't have fear at this point; rather, he was focused solely on how to survive. Perhaps he could grab the officer when he came back. The shelling continued nearby. Maybe an errant shell would save him, one way or another.

Gruber turned from the group and walked back to Cullerton, pointing Bill's own .45 at him. The officer motioned for everyone to move back into the forest. Shells continued to explode, and the thundering of explosions was merely background noise to Cullerton now. Colonel Gruber yelled *"Halt!"* They all stopped and Cullerton turned to face the officer. Without hesitation or remorse, the German brought Cullerton's own gun to bear on him. Bill knew it was coming. Coldly Gruber spoke, "American, you killed my parents, my brother, and my hounds. Now I will kill you."

The left-handed SS officer calmly aimed point-blank at Cullerton's midsection from eighteen inches away and said in accented English, "For you, the war is over," and pulled the trigger as Cullerton's right leg moved back in instinctive anticipation. Those were to be the last words Cullerton would ever hear.

The .45 caliber round pierced Cullerton on his right side, just below his rib cage. The power of the round lifted him off the ground, as the last bullet from his own gun channeled through his back.

He spun in the air and landed on his backside. He was out cold. Standing over Cullerton, the dispassionate Nazi pulled the trigger three times more; Bill's gun was empty. It wasn't much of a concern to the German, as a point-blank shot from a Colt .45 was always fatal. Another artillery shell exploded close by, sending the soldiers rushing toward the colonel. Gruber wanted to shoot Cullerton again with his own service pistol, but as another shell exploded even closer, the Germans staggered. Two of them helped Gruber up, as he had fallen to his knees. They went deeper into the woods, beyond harm's way. Gruber realized that he still had the American's gun; he smiled and slipped it in his pocket.

Cullerton lay motionless on the forest floor. The Germans moved on as he layed unconscious and bleeding heavily. Upon entering his body, the bullet had passed under his front ribs, piercing his lover like a doughnut and partially cauterized it on the way. The bullet nicked his kidney and cracked a back rib on its way out. As Gruber had pulled the trigger, Bill had moved his right foot slightly back in anticipation of the impending shot, changing the path of the bullet away from his spine. One bullet, two holes, and a lot of damage in between left Cullerton a hair's breadth away from death.

Through the centuries in Europe, and all of the battles fought over these godforsaken lands, how many soldiers had died on the fields and forests of battle from wounds incurred? If we were to look back two thousand years, the answer would probably be in the hundreds of thousands.

After Bill had lain unconscious for a few moments, the bleeding from both wounds began to slow. Some of the muscles in his stomach and back constricted, temporarily squeezing damaged blood vessels, and amazingly, his remaining blood began to clot. Cullerton had lost a lot of blood; he lay on the forest floor slipping in and out of a light coma throughout the night. The temperature dropped into the low forties. His extremities would not get frostbite at this temperature, but with the cold air, his metabolic rate would inevitably slow. Given a momentary opportunity, Bill's body slowly began trying to repair itself from what should have been a mortal wound.

> *Out of this wood do not desire to go*
> *Remain here, weather thou wilt or no*
> *Alas, young Sire, do not despair*
> *Renew thy Earth-bound temple*

In the Black Forest
April 14
Day 7 on the Run

The morning sun warmed the crypt-like forest air, and the sunlight cut through the leafless canopies above, shining on Cullerton's closed eyes, while the breeze gently moved the great trees, and the flickering brightness tapped his closed eyes. The fluttering light sparked brain activity and Bill began to ascend from a deep painless place to a semiconscious state. He partially opened his eyes to the brightness and was only faintly aware of what had happened to him. He felt his midsection; it was soaked with blood. He couldn't see it, but he felt his fingers become sticky as they dried. He rested his right hand on the wound, turned his head away from the sun, and slipped back into a deep, semi comatose sleep. The air remained cool, but the sun heated the cold coagulated blood on his jacket. The sun had shone all day and Cullerton's fragile body absorbed its brilliant offering. Bill lay motionless at the edge of a clearing on the forest floor. He felt at peace now.

The air war continued above, and the ground war continued around him. Cullerton was out of the way of retreating soldiers; Colonel Gruber had made sure of that. Bill lay in a gully, partially concealed; no one would ever find him here. As the sun set on a cloudless day, the warmth went with it, and Bill now faced his second night unprotected in the forest. He began to shiver. It was unlikely that two nights in a row would escape subfreezing temperatures, but Cullerton was still semicomatose, and he couldn't tell the difference.

The Reapers aura clings to the trees
And Sol's strength must slowly ease

A battle engages on the opaque stage
For the soul that lingers before Luna's rage

Death moves nearer in an icy veil
And a broken wing prepares to sail

Yet the dragon's blue breath follows near
To chase the chill, still air malevolent here

Be gone now, Death, and do not tarry
There will be no passenger tonight on Charon's Ferry

In the Black Forest
April 15
Day 8 on the Run

During the cool, clear night on the fourteenth of April, an air stream from the Mediterranean pushed northward and warmed the forest floor. It became a beautiful early spring day in the Black Forest for the second day in a row. Again the strobe-light effects of the sun filtered through the leafless canopy to alert the semi comatose pilot. Cullerton opened his eyes to the sun. He was surprised to feel the rays, and he wondered how long he had been out. He then remembered that he had been shot, so he felt his jacket at the site of the wound. His coat was crusted on top and only slightly damp at his back. Bill did not lift his head; he only rolled it from side to side, looking around with his eyes. He could see nothing but leafless trees. As Cullerton lay there, he tried to recall any recent events and figure out his options for survival. In his jacket pocket he felt a chunk of potato. Without hesitating or even taking a look, he put it in his mouth and devoured it. He felt stronger today than he had the last time he'd been awake, so he moved his arms out to scrape in as much brush as he could to cover himself. He still felt very cold and couldn't imagine ever feeling warm again; moving the brush against his body was a vain effort to retain any heat.

The grounded pilot was once again fatigued, so he closed his eyes and slipped back into a nether world between sleep and waking. Cullerton's body was fragile as it slowly continued to heal itself. He slept the rest of the day, and fortunately, the temperature did not go below forty degrees that night.

A Chance

April 16
Day 9 on the Run

Outside of the German town of Feuchtwangen, old-timer Erwin Strobel walked alongside his donkey. They were following his dog, which was on a scent trail, and the donkey pulled a two-wheel cart. Except for the aircraft flying overhead, this was a scene out of the Middle Ages.

Erwin, now close to seventy years old, had once been an honest and honorable man. He had been a stone and brick mason, one of the best around. These days, however, times were hard for him. He was growing older and didn't care much about the war, as he spent his days struggling to find food. He had even started to rob dead bodies for anything of worth that he could sell. *Maybe the Americans will bring food with them when they come*, he thought. He had a wife and a grandchild left to support. His one son and one daughter had moved to Berlin in 1941 to fulfill their patriotic duty for the Fatherland. Erwin had not heard from either of them since they'd come to visit at Christmas in 1943. Erwin and his wife now cared for their only daughter's child. It was supposed to have been for a month, but their daughter had never returned for her. He was sure that his children were dead.

The war had reduced Erwin to a shell of what he once was. Slowly he and his cart moved into the forest. The dog had found something; he did not bark but sniffed excitedly. The dog was trained that way because Erwin didn't want to alert others and have to share his findings. As Erwin approached, he saw the body on the ground. The dog stood next to the body, wagging his tail.

Erwin and his donkey pulled the cart closer, and he walked over to the body of the dead soldier. As he started to rifle through the dead man's pockets, he noticed the young man's chest rise and fall, and he realized that this soldier was not dead. Nevertheless, Stroble continued to rifle through the soldier's pockets. He thought to himself, *Well, this is not an infantry soldier, wearing these clothes, and he certainly isn't a German soldier. Hmm, and luckily, the Americans and British aren't anywhere around here yet.* He found nothing in the pockets or tucked into his socks and shoes. He sat down, pondered the situation, and came to the conclusion that this was a *Deutsche Flieger*, a German pilot. This was good news indeed. Erwin knew that if he brought in a wounded German pilot, he would surely be rewarded. "What a find," he said to himself as he continued to search for valuables.

He didn't see the gold chain and crucifix around the pilot's blood stained neck, because the wounded man was buttoned all the way up. Erwin found a compass, matches, some sunglasses, and that was about it. *Yes, this is a pilot,* he thought. There was something in the man's shirt pocket, but the pocket had a bullet hole in it, and the item was stuck in the blood. Erwin decided to leave it alone in case it was the man's ID. He didn't want to be accused of stealing. The card was bloody anyway.

Strobel positioned the cart as close to the body as he could and lifted the cold, unconscious airman into it. Strobel noticed that the man began to bleed from his stomach wound, so on the journey to the hospital in the nearby town of Feuchtwangen, Strobel stopped to check on his prize several times. He was as careful as he could be; a dead German pilot would not get him any reward. In fact, he could be shot for being a nuisance to the German military.

Although Strobel didn't know it at the time, Bill had been slightly conscious while the German was going through his pockets. Bill was a bit twitchy about interacting with any Germans but didn't have the strength to resist the man anyway. The German hadn't killed him, however, so Bill felt that he might get medical help after all.

The pain had been excruciating as the old man had lifted him into the back of the cart, but Cullerton hadn't reacted. As Bill grappled with what was happening, he decided that this was better than lying on the forest floor, and that it was better than the alternative.

Needless to say, every bump and rut of the cart ride jerked and tugged at the open wound. It was very dangerous until the cart had made it back to the smoother part of the road. After a few minutes, Cullerton slipped back to semiconsciousness, which helped to dull the pain.

"Sprechen Sie Deutsch?"

April 17
The Town of Feuchtwangen
Day 10 on the Run

Feuchtwangen was a small city in southern Germany which dated back to the 12th century. It had once been a walled city and was now a city of of over five thousand people. The famous medieval village of Dinkelsbuhl was just down the road. Feuchtwangen was more of a farm town than an industrial town, and it was just large enough to have a small hospital. Even though it had never been bombed, the town had come to very bad times with the war. With the beautiful Bavarian-style buildings and cobblestone streets, a visitor here would half expect to see Heidi and Grandfather walking down the hill. But that vision was long gone, because if you were to see Heidi walking down the street these days, she would be dressed as a Hitler youth in black jumper, white blouse, and black beret. She would have a Luger pistol in one hand and a Hitler youth knife in the other and be on her way back from having Grandfather "reassigned" to some labor camp.

Feuchtwangen was a very active town at the end of the war, with the influx of the civilian refugees from the east mostly, but now also from the west. A battalion of the regular German Army was stationed there, and the wounded German soldiers from the Russian front were convalescing in the ill-equipped hospital. To make matters tenser, the Americans were now a few miles to the north and moving closer to the town every day. Refugees from the countryside to the north, west, and south were all migrating into town ahead of the Allied advance.

After four hours of foot travel, Erwin, along with his dog, donkey, cart, and his prize, were reaching the outskirts of the east side of Feuchtwangen. Strobel had partially covered Cullerton with a burlap bag and straw; not out of the goodness of his heart; he just didn't want anybody to spot a soldier in his cart and take away his fortune. It was a smart move, since many military vehicles passed him by on the road into town. At this point, nobody cared about what was in Strobel's cart.

Cullerton, who had flown over this very town at four hundred miles an hour in the world's fastest warplane only a few days ago, now entered the town on the bed of a donkey cart, semiconscious and gravely wounded, bleeding on a bed of hay. The irony was compelling as the American warplanes flew overhead to a destination farther east, and Bill was very aware of this paradox as he spit hay out of his mouth.

When Cullerton and his medieval entourage reached the hospital, the old German checked again to see if Cullerton was still alive and then proceeded to go inside for help. Soon, the hospital staff came out to bring the wounded *Deutsche Flieger* into the hospital on a wheeled stretcher.

As the nurses removed his flight jacket and unbuttoned his shirt, the doctor, Dr. Arthur Maier, closely examined his wounds. Dr. Maier knew right away that this wasn't a German flier. The doctor told the nurses, who were Lutheran nuns from a nearby convent, to put Bill's jacket under the gurney and to leave his clothes on. They were to clean and bandage the wounds and then cover him with blankets up to his neck. The doctor gave Cullerton two pills: one was an antibiotic and the other was a vitamin. One of the civilian nurses told the doctor that she thought the patient was English, or worse, an American. Maier nodded in agreement. He could do no more for Bill, or his own life would be on the line.

Bill half-opened his eyes. He was on a gurney in the middle of a hallway in a German hospital, surrounded by wounded German soldiers. His pulse pounded, and he could feel his heart thumping through his chest.

The nurses at the hospital liked Dr. Maier and didn't care that he was a Jew. They wouldn't tell the commanding German officer that Maier had treated the American, for they were compassionate about all wounded people. In fact, the nurses washed off Cullerton's face as he awakened and fed him some bread and water. But soon that would be all the treatment they could give him.

Maier had been taking care of wounded German soldiers for six years at various hospitals. He went where they told him without complaining, or he could end up at a labor camp. He knew what was coming with the arrival of this Allied soldier. Meanwhile, the peasant who had brought the flier in would want to speak to the officer in charge for his reward. Dr. Maier gave Strobel some of his own money and some hospital food and told him to get along. Strobel had thought there would be more, but he took what Maier gave him and left. By paying Strobel himself, Maier had hoped to buy the American some time and keep the German officers away from him, but word had already begun to spread throughout the hospital. It would only be a matter of time before someone in charge would arrive and inquire about the American on the gurney.

Dr. Maier approached the gurney upon which the wounded American lay, and the thirty-two-year-old, weary, brown-haired, brown-eyed doctor spoke in broken, German-accented English.

"Sind Sie Deutscher?"

Cullerton shook his head no.

"*Englander?*"

He shook it again.

"*Sind Sie Amerikaner?*"

Cullerton nodded affirmative.

Maier then noticed the gold cross on Cullerton's neck, which the body robber had missed.

"*Katholisch*, are you *Katholisch*?"

This time Bill answered in American English, since he had exhausted his knowledge of German.

"Yes, I am. Are you?"

"No, I am Jewish, and I am your friend." Maier responded.

Cullerton nodded again.

The doctor continued, "You are wounded badly and bleeding. You are going to die. Do you understand? I cannot repair your wound. You are bleeding to death."

Bill closed his eyes and considered what the doctor had said.

The doctor momentarily stepped away, and Cullerton's mind raced. He thought of the last time he had seen Steve at the train station in December and promised her that he would be back in May. He saw again her face. Then the vision of the Nazi who had shot him flashed through his mind. Now he began to remember lying on the forest floor. *No*, he thought. *No, goddamn it! I'm not going to die! Not now, not here.*

The doctor reappeared with a paper and a pencil and said to Cullerton, "Let me write a letter for you. To your mother or father, perhaps. What do you want to say . . . last words?"

With that. Cullerton gritted his teeth and said, "To hell with that." He reached over and grabbed the paper from the doctor and crumpled it up. This time Maier nodded. He admired the young man's courage, even though Dr. Maier knew it was in vain.

It was getting close to nighttime now, and Cullerton realized that this would be his first night indoors in a long time. He couldn't recall how long it had been. In fact, Cullerton didn't know which day of the week it was, let alone the date.

A janitor at the hospital, a German citizen and rabid Nazi, observed all of this. He moved over to Cullerton's gurney and bent forward over Bill. He looked Cullerton in the eye and moved his right index finger across his own throat and then pointed his finger at Bill and grinned. Cullerton stared back; then the janitor turned away, sardonically smiling, and skulked down the hallway.

At that moment, a German Army captain approached Maier, who was standing near the gurney. *"Herr Doktor, dies ist der Amerikaner?"* he said to Dr. Maier.

"Ja," replied the doctor, with his hands in his pockets and his bloodstained coat open. "This is the American." The captain, along with three soldiers, wanted to take Cullerton right then. Dr. Maier gently argued with the captain that he not take the American, as he would not live through the night and was also delirious. The German officer refused; he and three other soldiers decided they would take Cullerton.

As the captain began to motion to the soldiers, Dr. Maier took a big chance and said, "If you take him, you'll have to sign for him. Those are the rules. We've already admitted him to the hospital. He is in the record." He hadn't really signed Bill in yet, and the German captain wouldn't sign for him.

"Captain," Maier continued, "the Americans will be here soon and they will be looking for him, and they will want to see our records."

At this, the German captain stopped and looked at the wounded American.

"All right, Doctor, I will leave him with you, but no one is to feed this son of a bitch, and no one is to treat him, either. He better die tonight." Bill was listening with his eyes closed and sensed the drift of the conversation.

At this point, Cullerton would have preferred to be alone under a pine tree, freezing his ass off.

The German captain left. For the first time since he had been shot, Cullerton was fully alert. *How the hell am I going to get out of here?* he wondered. Maier nodded to his patient, as Bill nodded back his thanks. Bill knew that he had dodged death again and that Maier had risked his life for him.

Maier put Bill in a small storage room and had an orderly hang around as a guard outside. Maier didn't want someone walking by, especially the janitor, and cutting Cullerton's throat during the night. Once he was in his room, Bill knew he had to get mobile very fast. As soon as he was alone, he started to move his legs around. He started flexing his arm and leg muscles. He hadn't stood on his feet in more than three days. He became hungry again, and then a little Dutch kid who acted as a hospital orderly slipped into his room. The boy couldn't have been older than ten. The kid waved to him, went over to him, and gave him a piece of bread and a handful of nuts. "Thank you," Bill said, and the youngster smiled, waved, and slipped out of the room. The boy reappeared a few minutes later with a glass of water. He waited for Bill to drink it all, then recovered the glass and slipped out again.

After the boy had left, the Nazi janitor slipped in. Cullerton braced himself as the Nazi moved toward him, speaking angrily in German. Just as Cullerton began to plan his attack strategy, a woman walked into the room with a warm homemade cherry pudding. She said hello to the janitor, and then he left the room. The sweet woman had just saved Bill's life, and she didn't even realize it. Bill took a bite of the cherry pudding; it was the first warm food he had tasted in ten days. He thanked the grandmotherly woman, saying *"Danke, danke"*; she patted his hand while he thanked her.

Bill was energized by the lurking janitor, the sweet German lady, and the desire to escape once again. He was determined to prove the doctor wrong by not dying; Cullerton pulled himself up into a sitting position. He checked the wound and saw only a little blood. He was feeling better, but his entire body hurt. He turned himself in the bed and dangled his legs off the side. He had to try to stand up. Bracing himself, he began to shift his weight to one leg. "Still okay; no major bleeding." He finally stood on both feet, but leaning on the bed. He was very dizzy at first and his legs were rubbery, but he was standing. Now that he knew he could get up onto his feet, he felt better about his chances of survival. After a minute or so, he rolled back onto the bed on his side, exhausted. Cullerton let himself fall back to sleep.

Hospital Time

April 18
Feuchtwangen Hospital
Day 11 on the Run

These were terrible times for all German citizens, and protecting children was especially difficult. As the war began to turn against Germany in 1943, many families sent their young girls to rural convents for safety. In the mountains near Feuchtwangen there was a Lutheran convent. Since most trained German medical personnel were conscripted to various fields of battle on the Eastern and Western Fronts, the local military ordered the convent to provide medical assistance at Feuchtwangen Hospital. Many of these young girls, who had been sent to the convent for safekeeping, were now medically trained novice nuns and worked in this and other beleaguered hospitals.

All hospital staff and the "volunteer" nurses from the convent were aware that the American pilot was not to be treated or fed. He was to be left to die. During the night, the hospital staff was to check on the American only to see if he was dead. Dr. Maier's orderly had been replaced by an older man who had been conscripted into the Home Guard. The guard was posted outside of the storage room, and his job was to search everyone who wanted to enter for food or medicine. The man was indifferent to the American, but he had a job to do.

Late in the evening, a young nun approached to enter the room. The guard stopped her and, as he'd been told to do, asked her reason for entry. She told the guard that she needed to grab some supplies. He searched her in a gingerly, but respectable, way, let her in, and closed the door. As soon as she got inside of the storage room, she went over to Cullerton's gurney and attempted to wake him. As he came to, she motioned "shhhh," to him with her finger over his mouth.

In a sweet twist of fate, the quasi-military guard refused to let the janitor into Cullerton's room.

Cullerton awakened and looked at the nun, and from his prone position, she was a vision. With her back to the door and facing Cullerton, she began to lift her skirt in the front. Cullerton's eyes became saucerlike; he could not believe what he was seeing. He looked at her face and realized that this wasn't a typical nun; she was about nineteen years old and, as far as he could tell, she was very pretty. He watched as, right out of the front of her bloomers, she brought a cooked potato. She smiled, put it under his pillow, walked over to the shelves to grab some sheets, and left the room. Cullerton waited a moment and then devoured the potato.

He looked down at his wound as he lay back down. He noticed that he was still in his clothes, and that his flight jacket remained hooked underneath the gurney. Beneath the blankets, his bleeding had stopped, and his wounds continued to heal. He moved his legs around and flexed his legs to stimulate circulation. He got out of bed and took a few steps; his strength was beginning to return.

Dr. Maier stayed at the hospital that night and attended to all of his German military patients. He did not want anyone to know of his concern for the American and his arrangements with other staff to keep him alive. With the new guard posted outside of Cullerton's room, Dr. Maier would not go in. He was still afraid that Cullerton would die in the middle of the night, although if he did not bleed out, he might actually have a chance, that is, if the German guard didn't slip in and kill him on his own.

April 19
Feuchtwangen Hospital
Day 12 on the Run

Bill did not wake up until about 9:00 a.m. The gurney had felt like the best bed in the Palmer House or the Ambassador Hotel in Chicago. He checked under his pillow. There were two rolls and an apple. The Sisters of Mercy had come again during the night. Cullerton's spirits rose. He looked down at his wound. After taking a few more steps around his room, and finding a steel bed pan, he got back on his gurney. There was no extensive bleeding and no internal pains to speak of. He then laid back down in relief.

Cullerton lay on the gurney, wide awake. His mind flooded with thoughts now. He thought about Steeple Morden. He knew that his fighter squadron was somewhere overhead at this very moment, escorting the "Big Friends" or strafing the Germans somewhere. Of course, he had no idea that the air war over Europe was only hours away from being over. He realized that the Army probably thought he was dead, and he had become just another statistic. His mind raced, and he thought about Steve. Steve must have gotten the news by now. He wondered whether the Army had listed him as Missing in Action or Killed in Action. In addition to feeling alone, he now felt terrible to think of the pain that his family and Elaine must have been in. Yet, here he was, a wounded prisoner, in the middle of Germany, still alive. *How the hell can I get out of here?* he thought. He had survived this far, and he was more determined than ever to make it home.

Then, as if on cue, the German captain from the previous day burst through the door. He came over to see if the American was still alive. The German spoke in broken, but clear, English. "So, you have not died, as *Herr Doktor* predicted?" The captain motioned to two uniformed privates to pick up the American. They pulled Cullerton off the gurney and leaned him against a wall next to a stairway leading down to a cellar. Cullerton was dressed except for his shoes and his flight jacket. He wore his blood-soaked shirt with the two bullet holes and his new captain's bars on it. It was tucked in. He was as presentable as an officer could be under these circumstances.

The two captains looked at each other, eye to eye. Cullerton's pulse raced; he tried not to show the excruciating pain from being muscled by the soldiers. The last time he'd looked a German officer in the eye, the guy had shot him.

"What is your *namen, Rang, und Serriennummer*?"

It was an order, not a question.

Cullerton responded, "Cullerton, William J., Captain, United States Army Air Corps, 0.7.0.6.3.6.0."

"An American behind the lines? You must be a spy or a pilot."

"I'm no spy."

"Are you a *Flieger*? Where are you based?"

No answer.

"Which fighter group or bomber group is yours?"

No answer.

"No matter, Captain, have you not heard? Roosevelt is dead. Your countrymen have lost the will to fight."

"Then we'll just have to let Stalin finish you sons of bitches off," Bill quipped.

This agitated the German even more, and with that, he grabbed Cullerton, punched him in the face, and pushed him down the stairs to the cellar. Cullerton was conscious, but blacked out momentarily from the fall. He was bleeding again from his stomach wound and that made Cullerton furious. He was fed up with Germany and all of the Germans in it.

Dr. Maier had been anxiously stalling outside Cullerton's room after he saw the soldiers enter. When Maier heard the noise, he rushed in. "Captain, Captain," he pleaded.

The two soldiers brought Cullerton back up the stairs. At the top, Cullerton pushed them away and stood there facing all of the Germans, including the doctor. Bleeding, frustrated, and angered, Cullerton said to the German officer, "The only thing that I will discuss with you, sir, is the unconditional surrender of this damn town. You are finished!"

The German captain stood there, enraged. Dr. Maier was shocked. Eighteen hours ago he had thought this American would be dead. Now here he was, bleeding and alone, and demanding the German surrender of the town. The German reached for his sidearm. Maier pressed his luck and physically restrained the German officer, and was gut-punched by a soldier. Maier doubled over, powerless.

"Captain, he must be delirious. Look, he is bleeding; he will die." The Germans stared at Maier as he pleaded; they glared at Cullerton, turned and left the room.

Once outside of the storage room, the German captain ordered his soldiers to move on. He told Dr. Maier that someone would be back for the American the next morning, since the Army was pulling out of town and heading north. Maier could only nod in acknowledgment. Amazingly, no guards were posted outside of the storage room.

After the Germans left with Dr. Maier, Cullerton struggled to get back on the gurney. He almost passed out again. He lay there, breathing heavily and bleeding from the gut, his back, and his lip. Cullerton's involuntary trip down the stairs had caused some setbacks to his recovery. But Bill knew that he could move around and perhaps get out of Feuchtwangen that night. It was time to go;

the good news that the Army was leaving seemed to have been passed around.

Late in the afternoon, any German soldiers that could walk or hobble were released from the hospital. The evacuation was beginning.

The little Dutch boy was looking for Dr. Maier, and he was in a hurry. The youngster told the doctor that he'd heard the Germans were going to come for the American in the middle of the night, not the next morning, and they weren't going to sign anything. Maier thought for a moment. Then he gave the boy some money and instructed him to pay a sheep farmer to dump three piles of manure on the ground outside of a particular window of the hospital. It was a room in the back, away from the street. The boy immediately set out on his mission.

After all of the evacuation activity around Cullerton's room began to quiet down, the doctor slipped in.

"American, you are in trouble."

Cullerton closed his eyes and thought to himself, *This isn't news.*

"The army is withdrawing from town, and the soldiers will come for you tonight. They will take you with them and they will kill you outside of town. I won't be there to stop them. I wouldn't be able to stop them even if I were there." As Cullerton began thinking of his options, the doctor told him of his own plan.

With fresh blankets on the gurney, two nuns wheeled Cullerton to a newly available room in the back of the hospital. They put some food into the pockets of his bullet-holed, bloodstained leather flight jacket.

Around 10:00 p.m., Dr. Maier completed his rounds as his shift ended in the now-empty hospital. When he finished writing reports in medical charts, he and the Dutch orderly went into Cullerton's new room for the last time. The boy put a piece of bread into Cullerton's hand and hugged the American. After the hug, Bill saluted the youngster, who stood at attention and saluted back. The boy then went over to the window and opened it slightly to make sure it was operable.

Dr. Maier looked at Cullerton's wound as he sat on the edge of the bed. Maier had never seen anything like it before; the bleeding had stopped again and the wound was healing on its own. Dr. Maier gave Cullerton some newspaper for packing his woulnd and examined him. He reasoned that as the bullet passed through Cullerton it had only damaged and not destroyed any major organs. As for his not bleeding out, he couldn't explain that. The doctor washed Bill's wounds and tied newspaper bandages over the entry and exit holes. Medically, that was all he could do. Cullerton slowly tucked in his bloody shirt as Maier helped him on with his bloody flight jacket.

"American, in an hour or so, when it is completely dark, you must leave here through this window."

"Okay, Doc, but that's a long five feet down, out that window."

"I have taken care of that. Just roll out into the manure. It will break your fall."

"I'm jumping into manure, eh Doc?" Cullerton laughed, shook his head, and muttered something to himself. "Thank you . . . for everything."

Cullerton stood up and shook hands firmly with the doctor. He thanked Dr. Maier for risking his life to save him. Maier hugged Bill. Cullerton again, thanked the boy, who was still nearby, and shook his hand, but the boy hugged Bill again, as the doctor had.

Dr. Maier and the Dutch orderly left the room and turned out the light. Bill was on his own again. He sat in the room, knowing that the soldiers would be back for him at any time. He was nervous and couldn't sit much longer, but he waited until it was quiet outside. He got up, zipped up his flight jacket, and painfully moved to the window. He opened it up enough to roll out of it and let himself fall into the pile of sheep manure. He was in it again; this time, literally.

Cullerton hit the pile hard on his back. He didn't have to look down; he knew that he was bleeding again. The pain. The smell. Which was worse? He rolled off the manure pile and bent over to relieve some of the pain, as he began to move toward the west side of town. It took stealth not to make any noise while maneuvering through town, but he finally made it to the western edge. He saw a flowing stream with a strong stone bridge over it, about five hundred yards outside of town. He was sure that this was the main road in from the west. Cullerton's luck in the woods hadn't been the best on this trip, so he made the decision to hole up under the bridge. He gambled on waiting it out, since he had some food with him. He figured that he could hold out a day or two and wait for the Allied advance. The Americans might bypass this little town altogether, but the one thing Bill was sure of was that he couldn't go much farther on foot. He would have to stay under the bridge. He would stay there just like some damn troll in a Grimm's fairy tale; maybe he would pop out and scare someone.

Up and under the bridge he went. The air was cold, and it would probably get even colder. Even better news was that it began to rain. The cold and flu season had come to south Germany.

The Bridge Troll

April 20
Outside Feuchtwangen
Day 13 on the Run

Cullerton awoke under the bridge, and he was shivering. Once again his eyes were frozen shut. When he opened them, he could see that it was daylight outside of the bridge's cover. Although he was thirsty and sitting only a few feet away from fresh running water, Bill dared not move into the gray light of day. He had to remain under the bridge in the cold, damp recesses of the stone. It was an open-air tomb, but safe for the moment, and Bill was awake and alert. He ate some of the food he'd been given in the hospital. As he ate, he continued to wonder if he should risk drinking the water without his halazone tablets. He wasn't sure it was worth it. About the only thing he didn't have at this point was dysentery, so he decided against it. He could see the water, he could hear the water, and he could touch it, yet he was unwilling to drink it or fish in it. Oh, the torture. Bill tried to think of other things. He decided he would rather be thirsty than pay the consequences. He sat there for hours, and then he heard the distinct sounds of motors, and they were getting closer.

The motors he heard above didn't sound like the ones from Detroit. For three hours or so, trucks, tanks, cars, all types of vehicles, and soldiers on foot passed over the bridge. Cullerton was sure that it was a retreating German column. He listened and sometimes he heard voices; none of them were speaking in English. It was a continuous column, and fortunately, the retreating column did not stop on or near the bridge. After the Germans passed by, it was quiet again. Another day was ending, as he could see by the bridge shadow growing longer in the east as the sun set. His second night under the bridge began, and he was freezing again. Bill looked around. Fortunately, there were no other trolls looking for shelter. He was almost out of food, and he was hungry, much beyond the roll or two that he still had left, and he was thirsty as well. Bill was cold and his body hurt, but he was alive, and he believed the worst had passed. He held onto the hope that sometime soon the Americans would come down the road on which the Germans had just retreated. As his discomfort grew, so did his determination to complete his journey. He had come this far, he had been through too much, and he would not give up now. He had to get back home, and he would face each night as it came.

SCHEMATIC POSITIONS OF ALLIED & GERMAN ARMIES ON 4/21/45 (The day Cullerton was rescued.)

 **GERMAN CONTROLLED TERRITORY**

I'm an American

April 21
Under the Bridge
Day 14 on the Run

A sunny day knocked on Cullerton's bridge. But just like the day before, he could not go out and enjoy it. The foot and motor traffic over the bridge had been steady all night. It was still too dangerous. In the late morning, he heard people crossing the bridge. He didn't think they were military. They were probably German civilians, refugees now. Maybe this meant that the Americans were close behind. Cullerton's spirits rose and he felt energized. He was sure that today would be the day he would get to safety. He would let the Americans cross the bridge if they would get him the hell out of Germany.

Four Miles Northwest of Feuchtwangen

A convoy of American tanks, Army half-tracks, and hundreds of GIs was moving east, headed for another German city down the road. This was a spearhead of the US Twelfth Armored Division. They were on a roll; in fact, they were on a stampede. The Twelfth was at least five miles ahead of the main force, and they were going to keep moving forward.

Moving east along the highway toward Feuchtwangen, the convoy came under machine gun fire from the woods. The lead vehicles in the convoy weren't hit, but the tenth tank back was. The convoy stopped. Tank turrets turned toward the protective woods. Machine guns fired. There was a two-minute exchange of fire, and then it was over. Soldiers went into the woods to confirm that the ambushing Germans were dead. Sergeant James Washington came out of the woods and went back to the tenth tank. The rig was okay, but the machine gunner on the top-mounted .50 caliber had been killed. The gunner, Sergeant Ronnie Jones, who had been shot between the eyes, had been Jim's best friend. Jim was visibly shaken, and now his anger became fury. Captain Sullivan went over to calm the sergeant down. Jim and Ronnie had been through the entire assault on fortress Europe together since D-Day.

Sergeants Ronnie Jones and Jimmy Washington made a strange pair. Jones was a white kid from a poor southern family, and Washington was a black kid, and from a well-to-do family out of Cleveland. Jim put his Thompson submachine gun down and took the top position on the mounted .50 caliber gun. He was pissed and fully intent on shooting anything that moved, civilian or military, whatever came across his gun sights was as good as dead. Inside Germany, everyone posed a threat to your life. He would shoot first and ask questions later. He didn't care whom he killed in Germany now.

Four Down The Road

It was getting to be late afternoon when Cullerton thought he heard it. It sounded like a Detroit motor. He didn't move but kept listening as he heard more vehicles drawing closer to the bridge. Bill looked out at the shadows as the vehicles passed over. He couldn't tell by the shadows, but he was sure that they were Detroit motors. He had to move out and see.

He eased himself down and moved out from under the bridge for the first time in almost sixty hours. As he came out into the sunlight, he rubbed his eyes and blinked. He held one hand over his wound and the other over his head; he began waving at the American convoy and yelling, "Hey, I'm American, American. I'm an American!"

Cullerton was looking into the sun, but he knew that they were US vehicles.

As the convoy moved over the bridge toward Feuchtwangen, the driver of the tenth tank in line saw someone emerge from under the stone bridge as his tank began to cross the bridge. Over his intercom, he alerted his inside machine gunner who had been looking in the other direction. The turret of the tank, big gun and all, swung around to where a figure, possibly a German soldier, had emerged from under the bridge. Jim considered that this was another German soldier with one of those damn potato masher hand grenades. Jim, on the top-mounted .50 caliber, immediately swung around, finger on the trigger. He spotted the figure next to the stream and he depressed the trigger to kill the waving soldier, now in his sights. He continued to swing the gun past the soldier and upward as he fired a quick burst. At the same time, he was yelling into his intercom to hold fire. He yelled down for the guy not to move. The bullets rushed past Cullerton.

"Dammit, I'm an American! American!" Cullerton yelled.

"We'll see, fella. Don't you move," said Jim, irritated and twitchy.

Two GIs ran over to the fellow in the bloody clothes, and it was confirmed, this was an American.

"Yep, he's an American, Sergeant," one of the soldiers yelled.

"A pilot. A captain," yelled the other.

Bill looked up at the black face of a very large US sergeant on a Patton tank, who was pointing a .50 caliber machine gun at his face. He saw the sergeant release his hand from the trigger, and Cullerton exhaled in relief. His fatigue and physical weakness overwhelmed his body now that he was in American hands, and he collapsed. The two GIs next to Bill caught him and carried him to the tank.

Jim, filled with anger, but with nerves of steel, slowly released his hand from the machine gun and looked up to the heavens. Jim breathed a nearly inaudible "Thank Christ!" How could he have lived with himself if he had killed an American by accident, and out of rage, no less.

Bill would never forget looking down the barrel of the .50 caliber gun and at the black face of the US sergeant who had aimed it at him. He exhaled in relief when the sergeant took his hand off the trigger as the two GIs helped him up from the river. The sergeant jumped off the tank and ran over to help the guys with Cullerton. Jimmy embraced Cullerton and thanked God he had not killed the wounded, emaciated pilot.

After thirteen days in hell, Cullerton was finally in the hands of the Americans. The GIs carried Bill to the medics and they looked at him closely, but they could only scratch their heads and clean his healing wounds. These medics had seen a lot of horror since D-Day, but they had never seen a point-blank through-and-through wound heal on its own. Needless to say, Cullerton was hungry, and the benevolent GIs decided to share their "liberated" brandy and half a dozen hard-boiled eggs with him. They all celebrated in great Army fashion that night, while they waited for proper medical treatment to arrive. Before the celebration, the Twelfth Armored commander wanted to debrief Bill about Feuchtwangen. Bill told the commander that the Germans were falling back out of the city and that the folks at the hospital needed to be protected, including Dr. Maier, the Lutheran nuns, and especially the Dutch kid.

Bill told the Americans about the janitor at the hospital and how he was a fanatical Nazi who had tried to kill him. Bill asked the guys to shoot the janitor, but he never received a follow-up on that request. However, there were several, very interested, American soldiers in the tent when Bill was being debriefed.

After the captain in charge of the spearhead had called his CO and informed him that they had picked up an American P-51 pilot, named Cullerton, of the 355th Fighter Group out of Steeple Morden, the military immediately notified Steeple Morden that Cullerton was alive and in American hands. The mood at the American air base in England was one of euphoria. They had declared Cullerton dead a long time ago.

After confirming with the Twefth Armored that they did, in fact, have Captain William J. Cullerton in their safekeeping, Bill's commanding officer at Steeple Morden called Bill's family to let them know their son was safe. At the same time, the war correspondents from Chicago were calling all of the newspapers back home about the miraculous return of their hometown hero.

With The Americans
Outside Feuchtwangen
April 21, 1945

The column had been ordered to stop outside of Feuchtwangen and set up camp for the night. This would give the Germans a chance to get out of town and give the column a chance to prepare for a peaceful entrance to Feuchtwangen or a bloody assault the next day.

A doctor had been brought up from the rear to help with Bill's wounds. After arriving at the outskirts of Feuchtwangen at first light on the morning of April 21, the doctor, a major, looked over his new patient. He had come to treat Cullerton and to bring him back to the US Army field hospital outside of Paris. Bill was nearly comatose. "Jesus Christ!" barked the angry major. "You sons of bitches got this guy drunk." The soldiers stood around kicking the dirt in the tent. They made sideways glances at each other while avoiding eye contact with the major.

The doctor shook his head. "Are you guys trying to kill him? Look at his wounds."

Cullerton lay on a cot in the tent, completely drunk. As everyone watched, Bill rolled to his side and started throwing up on the tent floor. The GIs laughed.

"Shut the hell up! Get out of the tent!" the major ordered.

They all stood at attention while the MPs and medical group loaded the wounded, drunk, and vomiting pilot into the ambulance for the six-hour express ride back to the American Field Hospital based on the outskirts of Paris. Cullerton waved a weak goodbye, and the GIs waved back, wishing him well and cheering him on. Despite the gunshot wound, despite his headache and upset stomach, Cullerton had never felt better.

US Eighth Air Force HQ
England
May 1945

The word of Cullerton's safe return got back to the executive offices at Eighth AF HQ. General Doolittle was relieved, very relieved, to get his second-highest-scoring strafer in the entire Eighth AF back. Since the eighth of April, both Captain Bill Cullerton and Colonel Elwyn Righetti had been shot down while strafing. Righetti was the leading strafer, with twenty-seven ground kills, and Cullerton was second at the time, with twenty-one ground kills. Major John Landers and Captain John Thury, the other two leading strafers in the Eighth Air Force, were still okay.

General Doolittle ordered the cessation of all strafing by midmonth in April 1945. Cullerton was one of the last eight pilots who had been lost in April. The eight losses were in the 355th Fighter Group alone and were due to flak from strafing. After April 20, 1945, the day Cullerton was rescued, all offensive air operations in Germany were suspended.

General Doolittle's concern for his pilots was well known. Doolittle was proud of all of his pilots, but he had a special admiration for his strafers. The strafers faced such daunting odds in regard to their own survival. When Cullerton had gone down on April 8 and then Righetti on April 17, so close to the end of the war, Doolittle had been miserable.

Sadly, General Doolittle would not receive the same good news about Righetti that he had with Cullerton. Colonel Righetti, who had safely landed his damaged P-51 in a field outside of Dresden, was taken prisoner by German civilians. The civilians killed Righetti, even though he had surrendered as a prisoner of war. Within weeks of Righetti's execution by the Germans, Americans were hunting down the murderers. When caught, the German criminals were executed. But it would not bring back the well-liked and well-respected Elwyn Righetti.

Prisoner in Paris

American Field Hospital, Paris
May 1, 1945

Captain Cullerton was rushed to the US Army Field Hospital outside of Paris and was admitted on April 21. With regular food and good medical treatment, his body began to heal quickly. The surgeons did not operate on the captain, as his wound had already healed itself. The first thing the young captain did was to write a lengthy letter to his folks at home telling them not to worry and apologizing for putting them through so much anxiety. After a week or so, Cullerton was getting restless; he wanted to get back to England and Steeple Morden. He had asked to be released many times, but the hospital had rules; they told him he had to remain there for at least thirty days. Bill had an idea that might get him released. He wrote and sent an urgent letter to General Doolittle:

From:

>Captain Wm. J. Cullerton, 355th FIGHTER GROUP, 357th FS, Eighth Air Force

To:

>General James A. Doolittle, Commander, Eighth Air Force

General,

>Could you please send help? I'm being held prisoner by the US Army at the 250th Paris Field Hospital. I assure you that I am ready for travel.

Signed

>Cullerton, Wm. J., Captain, 357th FS, 355th FIGHTER GROUP

General Doolittle received Captain Cullerton's letter and was thoroughly amused. Doolittle sent his personal plane and adjutant to secure Bill's release from "American custody." Doolittle had Bill transferred to a civilian hospital, which the military also used, in Cambridge. At least he would be closer to his base while he recovered. Bill was very well known to Doolittle, and the general had watched Cullerton's progress.

While he was in Cambridge, many of the pilots and ground crew of the 355th came by to see Bill. His buddies Harry Spencer and Jack Crandell were among the first to visit, as well as Bert Marshall and Fred Havilland. The guys were all being reassigned, and they leaving Steeple Morden by the dozens every week. One day, the leading ace of the entire 355th FG stopped by. Henry Brown, who had twenty-eight and a half victories combined, along with another ace, Chuck Lenfest, stopped by to see Cullerton. Brown and Lenfest had just gotten back to Steeple Morden. They had become POWs in October of 1944, and now they were going home.

One day, Doolittle himself visited Cullerton. Bill was surprised and honored, and he saluted the general. Doolittle set him at ease as he sat and talked to the young captain.

He sat next to Bill's bed, listening intently as Bill relayed the story of his journey from Ansbach to Feuchtwangen. The general asked him some questions about the SS man who had shot him, and he told Bill that the Air Force investigators would pursue the matter and try to find out who he was. The general added, that, in all honesty, they would probably never get the guy. Cullerton understood, and he thanked the general for inquiring.

Doolittle also asked Cullerton about the four-day Warsaw Relief Mission in which Bill had participated, when the 355th FG had flown cover for the bombers. These bombers had supplied the Polish resistance who were trapped by the Nazis in the Warsaw ghetto. The Americans had had to fly to Russia for refueling before flying back to England, by way of Italy, to refuel there. Cullerton told the general that, while over Warsaw, they had seen the Soviet tanks poised to attack the Germans on a hill, but the Russians had never came to the aid of the Poles. Rather, the Russians had hung back and let the Polish resistance fighters be destroyed by the Germans. Bill and his Flight Group had flown over the Soviet tanks. Doolittle told Cullerton that the inaction of the Russians there was one of the many reasons that America would not ally with Russia after the war.

"It's all politics now, Bill," the general said.

"We felt like bombing the Russians at Warsaw, sir."

"I understand, Bill. I'm glad, though, that you didn't bomb or strafe the Russians."

The two men then briefly compared war wounds right there in the hospital ward. It was unusual to see a general untuck his shirt and pull it up to his chest, and Cullerton looked at the general's old wound. Doolittle conceded that Cullerton had the bragging rights on the wounds comparison. After looking closely at the entry and exit wounds, Doolittle pursed his lips and said, "Bill, one Purple Heart just doesn't seem like enough for this mess that you have here . . . Maybe two or three, or perhaps a giant Purple Heart!"

The general smiled and the two men laughed. Cullerton responded humbly, "General, sir, one purple heart is more than enough."

Doolittle nodded his head in admiration and continued to question Cullerton. "Bill, because of the severity of your wound, I don't see you receiving clearance to fly on active duty any time soon. But after the war, I am going to need a few personal pilots. Is flying for me something that you would be interested in doing?"

Cullerton was flattered. Doolittle told him, "We'll promote you to major right away and then to colonel in a couple of years, to get your pay grade up to where it should be."

"General, I don't know what to say. I never expected this. I am honored, extremely honored. Do you need an answer right now?"

"No, Bill. Sleep on it, and call me at this number in the next day or two."

Doolittle handed Cullerton his personal card and stood up as he prepared to bring their visit to a close.

"Thank you, sir, thank you very much."

"Make sure you let me know, Bill."

"I will, sir, thank you again."

Cullerton saluted the general, and General Doolittle returned the salute and extended his hand. The two men shook hands.

Bill was finally released from the hospital in Cambridge on May 31, and he took a cab out to Steeple Morden. As he drove through town along Hay Street, Cullerton's excitement waned as he realized that it was all over. The war was over. There were no more missions to fly, and the 355th FG had already been reassigned to Gablingen, Germany, as part of the occupation force. The base was being relocated, and Bill's spirits rose again when he realized that he would be going home to Chicago very soon.

Cullerton stepped out of the cab at the Steeple Morden Air Base, or at least what was left of it. He stood there alone, looking over the airfield. All that remained was a handful of Mustang aircraft and the wind blowing over the fields. He had stood at this same spot less than twelve months before, as a rookie pilot anxious to fly, with Mustangs parked all around and flying overhead. He walked out onto the runways and looked around. He realized that he would never fly here again. He looked out to where the hill dropped off.

Bill then walked over to the office of the squadron commander of the 357th FG. That was Captain John Elder, who had been his partner in the Switzerland mission. Bill stepped inside; an orderly and a sergeant were packing up the office. Cullerton inquired, "Excuse me, is Major Elder available?"

"No, sir," responded the orderly. "Major Elder has been reassigned to Gablingen. We're packing his office for shipment. The 357th Fighter Squadron has already left for Germany."

"Are you Captain Cullerton?" the sergeant asked.

"Yes."

"Captain, we were told to direct you to Colonel Kinnard's office for your orders."

"Thank you, Sergeant."

Cullerton returned salute, stepped out, and headed over to Colonel Claiborne Kinnard's office.

As the second-highest-scoring pilot, Colonel Kinnard had been promoted to Commander of the 355th Fighter Group. Henry Brown was the highest-scoring fighter in the 355th, and Cullerton was the next highest scorer after Kinnard.

"Captain Cullerton to see Colonel Kinnard."

"One moment, Captain."

The administrator let Cullerton into Kinnard's office.

"Cullerton reporting for duty, sir."

"Welcome back, Bill." Kinnard extended his hand to shake. "Bill, I have your orders here somewhere," he said. Kinnard looked around but couldn't find the paper.

"Essentially, you are on inactive duty now, and you get to go home for a ninety-day leave. The Army will know by then what to do with you, and you'll receive orders at your home then."

"I'm not going to Gablingen, sir, or maybe the Pacific?"

"No, Bill, for you the war is over."

That statement sounded better coming from Colonel Kinnard than it had from an SS officer. Bills mind drifted back as Kinnard continued to talk. The slight twinge of pain from the unhealed gunshot wound snapped Bill back into reality.

Kinnard was saying, "Enjoy your three months at home, Bill. Look, I'm going to give it to you straight. You've got a bad wound, and the Army now has a surplus of pilots with only half a war to fight. Your Army flying days are probably over. It is time that you go home, get married, and start a new life. You are a very lucky man."

"Thank you, Colonel. I realize that, sir."

As Cullerton turned and headed for the door, the colonel said one more thing. "Bill, you have been one of the best pilots in the 355th Fighter Group and in the Eighth Air Force. Remember that always, and thank you for your courage and leadership. I'm glad to have known you. If you ever need a recommendation, you can call me anytime."

"Thank you. Thank you very much, sir. I think I might need that recommendation."

"I'll have my assistant prepare one for you before you leave."

"Thank you, Colonel."

They saluted a "goodbye and good luck" salute.

Cullerton picked up his gear, which had been packed previously when everyone had thought him dead. He took what he could carry and then made one last trip around the base, carrying his gear all the while. He stopped and looked into the empty Ready Rooms. He went by the flight tower, a little two-story building. No one was there either. Finally, he stopped at the officers' club for one last drink. He saw some young pilots who had arrived in March or so. Bill didn't know them very well, but the two lieutenants came over to him and congratulated him on his safe homecoming. The three pilots toasted to the 355th FG, to the victory, and they briefly talked. Bill thanked the two pilots, wished them well, then shook their hands and said goodbye.

Bill left the officers' mess, reading his papers as he walked out. He was to catch a flight out of Bassingbourn, on a B-17, which was modified to carry soldiers heading back home. He had no reason to stay, except that he owed General Doolittle a telephone call. He could make that call from the active base at Bassingbourn as he waited for one of the three daily flights back to the States.

Cullerton hailed a jeep that was driving through the compound. He asked the driver if he could take him over to Bassingbourn. The sergeant gladly agreed, as he had a lot more time on his hands these days. When the young soldier helped Cullerton into the jeep, he noticed that Cullerton was moving somewhat tentatively; he knew about Cullerton's wound but didn't mention anything.

"How about a last look around, Captain?"

"That would be great, Sarge."

Sergeant Mike McCarthy knew the drill. He had driven many guys on a "last look" around both Litlington and Steeple Morden before they headed over to Bassingbourn. Their first stop was St. Catherine's Church in Litlington, a stone church that was nearly nine hundred years old. Sergeant McCarthy stopped the jeep; as both men looked up at the great steeple, a Mustang came toward the air base, circling around the great steeple. Bill and the sergeant looked at each other and nodded their heads. They drove on.

They passed the Crown Pub, but didn't stop as the jeep passed through Steeple Morden along Hay Street. Cullerton looked at the rural English cottages with thatched roofs. He saw the school and the playground packed with children. He waved to a local farmer who was making his way to the pub. The man waved back. Cullerton asked the sergeant to stop in front of a particular house, so McCarthy pulled over. Bill looked at the house. He had had dinner there a few times during the last year. A woman appeared in the doorway, and Bill waved. The woman came out.

"Lieutenant Cullerton, is that you?"

Mrs. Crow didn't realize that Cullerton had been promoted to captain. It didn't matter to Bill.

"Hello, Mrs. Crow."

"Are you all right, William? Don't get out of your jeep. We heard all about what those bloody Nazis did to you. It's a miracle, just a miracle, that you're alive and back home."

"Steeple Morden has been a wonderful home, Mrs. Crow. I'm fine now, thank you. Ma'am, I'm heading to the States today, and I wanted to say goodbye. I wanted to thank you for all of your hospitality this past year and also for having me over for dinner on several occasions."

"You're welcome, William. Some of the other gents have left and they stopped by to say goodbye as well. You know, we're going to miss all you Yanks. You've been a proper bunch. It's going to be different around here now. A bit lonely, I should think, and much quieter of course . . ." Her voice trailed off as she looked down the road.

"Is David around, ma'am?"

"No, William, he has gone to Cambridge with Father for the day."

"Will you tell him I stopped by to say goodbye?"

"Of course, William. He'll be extremely melancholy that he missed you."

Cullerton nodded his head to the kind woman and said, "Thank you, Mrs. Crow. I will always remember Steeple Morden fondly, and I'll never forget how you all made us feel at home here. I am going back to Chicago, and I'm gonna get married. Goodbye, ma'am."

"Good for you, Lieutenant. You deserve it. You marry the pretty lass with the lad's name. Godspeed now. Godspeed to all you Yanks." She reached into the jeep and gave the young American a hug.

As they drove off, Bill waved goodbye to Mrs. Crow. Bill could linger at Steeple Morden and Litlington no longer. It was time to go home.

On their ride over to Bassingbourn, the sergeant asked Cullerton a question. "Captain, which fighter squadron were you in?"

"The 3-5-7."

"Is that the group with the dragon mascot?"

"Yes . . . why do you ask?"

"Well, sir. You're the last one out."

"What do you mean, Sarge?"

"Captain, you are the last pilot of your fighter squadron to leave Steeple Morden. You are the last dragon." Cullerton did not say anything to him, but when the sergeant briefly turned to him, Bill tightened his lips and nodded in acknowledgment. The sergeant caught on to how emotional this was for Bill, and he nodded back.

As the two men rode off in silence, Cullerton realized that the separation from his home in England had become more difficult than he'd anticipated. He knew better than to look back. Even though it was a cloudy day, Bill donned his new sunglasses, which sure did come in handy.

Bill's Miliatry ID. It was in a leather sleeve in his shirt pocket when he was shot. Note the .45 caliber bullet hole in the upper right corner.

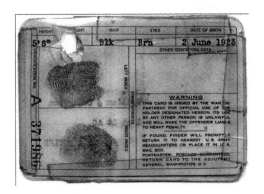

This is the backside view of Bill's Military ID card, with the bullet hole clearly visible.

Army of the United States

SEPARATION QUALIFICATION RECORD
SAVE THIS FORM. IT WILL NOT BE REPLACED IF LOST

This record of job assignments and special training received in the Army is furnished to the soldier when he leaves the service. In its preparation, information is taken from available Army records and supplemented by personal interview. The information about civilian education and work experience is based on the individual's own statements. The veteran may present this document to former employers, prospective employers, representatives of schools or colleges, or use it in any other way that may prove beneficial to him.

1. LAST NAME—FIRST NAME—MIDDLE INITIAL			MILITARY OCCUPATIONAL ASSIGNMENTS		
			10. MONTHS	11. GRADE	12. MILITARY OCCUPATIONAL SPECIALTY
CULLERTON, WILLIAM J.			1	Pvt	Basic 521
2. ARMY SERIAL NO.	3. GRADE	4. SOCIAL SECURITY NO.	22	Capt.	Pilot 1055
O 706 360	Capt.	Unknown	12	Capt.	Operations Officer
5. PERMANENT MAILING ADDRESS (Street, City, County, State)					
1719 New England Ave. Chicago, Ill.					
6. DATE OF ENTRY INTO ACTIVE SERVICE	7. DATE OF SEPARATION	8. DATE OF BIRTH			
10 Oct 42	9 Dec 45	2 June 43			
9. PLACE OF SEPARATION					
Amarillo Army Air Field, Texas					

SUMMARY OF MILITARY OCCUPATIONS
13. TITLE—DESCRIPTION—RELATED CIVILIAN OCCUPATION

Pilot - Single engine aircraft P-51, navigation, physics, mathematics, english and weather.

Flight leader in 8th Airforce. Awarded Air Medal and 7 clusters. Distingushed flying cross and 3 clusters. Silver Star, Distinguished Service Cross and Purple Heart.

WD AGO FORM 100
1 JUL 1945

This form supersedes WD AGO Form 100, 15 July 1944, which will not be used.

Bill's Army Discharge Certificate from December 1945. There was a surplus of pilots at this time, and Bill was considered "damaged goods," so he was Honorably Discharged.

Bill upon his arrival at Union Station in Chicago. (Left to Right) Bill's sister Jean, Elaine (Steve) Stephens, Bill, Bill's mother, and Bill's father Orville.

Steve and Bill on their wedding day, a mere
four months after his ordeal in Germany.

Picture Section
August 5, 1945
Chicago
Sunday
Tribune

STORY IN GRAPHIC SECTION   TRIBUNE COLOR STUDIO PHOTO

CAPT. WILLIAM J. CULLERTON, Chicago hero of the air. Top ranking pilot of the 335th fighter group, 8th air force, he is credited with 20 planes destroyed in the air and on the ground. Shot down over Germany, captured, shot by the enemy, he escaped and made his way to the American lines.

Chicago Tribune Magazine photo from August 1945.

Bill and friends in a sports gear promotional photo – circa the late 1960's.

Bill's official African Safari photo from 1969.

Fishing in the Caribbean in the 1980's.

Bill and Steve in the 1990's

Afterword

Since Bill had been the victim of a war crime—Attempted Execution—US Army Intelligence investigated the crime at the end of the war. But they were never able to locate any of the perpetrators. In time, the investigation was closed and life went on, as it always does. Bill became the third-highest Strafing Ace in the entire Eighth Air force (21 kills), behind Colonel Elwyn Righetti (27 kills) and Col. Joseph Thury (25.5 kills).

As Bill was mustering out of the Army at the end of 1945, he turned in all the gear that he had left, after his ordeal. In true Army fashion, the Army charged him $10 for his lost aviator glasses and $100 for his lost gun. No amount of explaining by Bill was going to get him off the hook. So the Army deducted the costs from his POW pay. Bill could only shake his head as walked out the door.

Bill married Elaine Stephen two weeks after arriving home in Chicago in 1945. They had five children together. The Cullertons had three girls and two boys, who they raised in Elmhurst, Illinois, west of Chicago. Their children, in turn, had nineteen grandchildren. Now those grandchildren are having children.

Bill remained in the sport-fishing business after the war and then started a manufacturers' representative company for sports equipment and gear in the 1950s. Bill was the sales representative, and Elaine ran the office from the family room in the back of their home in Elmhurst. Bill built his business on his knowledge of the outdoors, including fishing, camping, hunting, and athletics. Often, people who remembered Bill from the war would seek him out. Bill was honored that people would remember, and he was obliging if they had a question or two. He maintained his relationships with friends he had made at the different Chicago newspapers. Bill built his professional sports reputation on his abilities as a sport fisherman, salesman, and outdoorsman in general. One of Bill's great passions would be wildlife preservation and the preservation and conservation of natural habitats.

After the war, Bill's father, Orville, located Dr. Arthur Maier, who had treated Bill and saved his life at Feuchtwangen. Dr. Maier had gone back to Munich. To thank Dr. Maier, Orville sent him top-of-the-line surgical instruments, the best that money could buy. Orville passed away suddenly in 1948, and after that the Cullertons lost touch with Dr. Maier.

Bill kept in touch with Harry Spencer, who made a career out of the military and later retired back to the Chicago area. Harry Spencer taught Bill's grandson, Marc Brinkman, how to fly jets and Marc is now a commercial pilot.

Jack Crandell moved back to Aurora, Illinois, to start a family. He and Bill spoke occasionally over the years.

As time moved on after the war, and as the veterans' families grew up and moved on with their lives, the veterans began to reach retirement age. It was time for them to reflect back and consider their contributions during WWII that had brought peace and freedom to so many of the world's people. Veterans the world over began to contact one another, to form groups and rekindle relationships both at home and abroad.

So, every five or ten years or so, beginning in the 1980s, the veteran pilots, officers, and ground crewmen of the 355th Fighter Group reunited to catch up on old days and to reminisce and relive those times that changed the world so long ago. They reconnected with the townspeople of Litlington and Steeple Morden and contributed to various causes and projects in the two faraway towns.

Retired veterans of the Army, Navy, and Marines all over the world continue to meet and to remember a common call to a great cause and to share a story with someone who would care to listen, and to reinforce the point that good people cannot stand by and do nothing while evil is on the move.

Hopefully, we will never forget what the men and women of World War II fought for and what they achieved. Bill Cullerton's story is only one of thousands of great war stories; however, his personal experiences, of a high-flying aerial war and hand-to-hand combat in the Black Forest of Southern Germany in the closing days of the war, touch us viscerally and make his story compelling in the extreme.

Acknowledgments and Dedications

This is my first book and it has been one of the most difficult challenges I have ever attempted. Nevertheless, it has been an enjoyable journey to write this story—a couple of times.

I want to thank Bill and Elaine (Steve) Cullerton for allowing me to write Bill's story as a fighter pilot in WWII from 1942 to 1945. I would also like to thank their five children: Pamela (Cullerton) Brinkman, Cindy (Cullerton) Giesche, Bill F. Cullerton, Marc Cullerton, and Christine (Cullerton) Picchietti for their enthusiastic support in this effort.

My sons, Orion Kevil and John Kevil III, helped me research this project, and we accumulated quite a library among the three of us. Orion and John also provided written contributions to the story.

I thank my daughter, Hayley Kevil, for her editorial skills. I thank my Meaghan for her keying efforts.

I am grateful, especially, to my lifelong friend, Bill Cullerton, Jr., for his never-ending faith and encouragement.

Thank you to my wife, Donna, for her continuous support through many, many drafts and reading of the story.

I have written this story for a new generation of readers who did not grow up with the immediate experience of WWII as an integral part of their lives.

I hope you enjoyed this story, because it is true.

Glossary of Terms and Characters

Places (both home and abroad)

Ansbach

A city located in southern Germany, Ansbach was largely bypassed by the industrial revolution and remained a small town until after World War II.

Bassingbourn

A town in Southeast England, near Cambridge, Bassingbourn was a bomber base for the Eighth Air Force.

Bastogne

A city in Belgium, it was held by the US 101st Airborne during the German counteroffensive known as the Battle of the Bulge, in December 1944. Surrounded and cut off in the city of Bastogne, the isolated Americans refused to surrender, thereby bogging down the German counterattack.

Black Forest, The

The Black Forest (or Schwarzwald) is a section of southwestern Germany that borders Switzerland on the south, the Neckar River to the east, and France to the west. The Black Forest is the stage for many of the Brothers Grimm Fairy Tales. Culturally, the Black Forest is wrought with haunting and bad omens.

Dresden

A cultural center of Germany, Dresden was hit with five Allied air raids between February 13 and February 15, 1945. Fire destroyed most of the city, and over thirty-five thousand people died. It is located in east-central Germany.

Feuchtwangen

A city in the Ansbach district dating back to the mid 1100s, it had a population of about five thousand during WWII. As it was not an industrial center, it was largely untouched during the war, but Feuschtwangen had a hospital, which was commandeered by the German Army in 1945 and used as military hospital.

Littlington

This is the sister town to Steeple Morden. The 355th FG was based on the airfield between Littlington and Steeple Morden. The spire of St. Catherine's Cathedral in Littlington provided a landmark to the pilots upon their return flights. The cathedral was constructed approximately nine hundred years ago, yet in the chapel's Gothic-era limestone window frame, a stained glass window can be found dedicated to the 355th Fighter Group of the US Eighth Air Force during WWII.

Malmedy

A city in Belgium, Malmedy saw one of the terrible Nazi atrocities of WWII, the mass murder of the American POWs under Nazi control during the Battle of the Bulge. There is little known of this event, called the Malmedy Massacre. The shallow mass grave was uncovered in January of 1945 by the 291st Division of the Army Corp of Engineers. Accounts place the massacre at a month earlier.

Oak Park

This town, directly west and bordering on Chicago, is historically significant for producing great architecture (Frank Lloyd Wright and others) and writers (including Edgar Rice Burroughs and Ernest Hemingway). Oak Park is an affluent community and cultural center.

River Forest

A very affluent suburb of Oak Park and Chicago. One of the great towns of Cook County, it has been home to colorful Chicago gangsters, politicians, two private colleges and an all-girls, Catholic high school.

Steeple Morden

A small town near Cambridge England, founded in the twelfth century, Steeple Morden is rich in history and was home to the 355th FG and the Steeple Morden Airfield (a satellite of the Bassingbourn Airfield) and it was home to the RAF before that. The people of Steeple Morden still hold the American fighter pilots with highest regard.

People

Crandell, Jack

Lieutenant USAAF 357th FS. One Aerial Kill. Excellent pilot. Crandell's lone aerial kill saved Cullerton's life on August 16, 1944. (1.0 Aerial; 2.0 Ground).

Cullerton, Bill

Captain USAAF 357th FS. Subject of the story. Distinguished pilot who set several combat records including, the first Eighth AF pilot to destroy 7.0 aircraft in one day; the first Eighth AF pilot to destroy 8.0 aircraft in one day; First 355th Fighter Group pilot to destroy 15.0 aircraft on the ground. Final results: 6.0 Aerial; 21.0 Ground. Certified Aerial Ace and a quadruple Strafing Ace. Cullerton was the second-highest-scoring Strafing Ace in the entire Eighth AF. Top Ace in WWII in Chicago. Downed by ground fire, evaded capture, survived execution by SS.

Doolittle, James

General; Commander US Eighth Air Force 1944–1945. Distinguished leader and pilot; led the air raid on Tokyo, Japan, in 1942 with Air Force bombers off the US Aircraft Carrier Hornet. In 1944, in command of the Eighth AF, Doolittle ordered and encouraged strafing to strategically cripple the German capacity to wage war.

Gruber, Friedrich

German SS Officer who pursued Bill Cullerton through the Black Forest. Gruber is an amalgam of Nazi soldiers who pursued Bill.

Hauver, Charles

Lieutenant USAAF 354th FS. Achieved Ace Status (5.0 Aerial).

Havilland, Fred Jr.

Captain USAAF 357th FS. 357th FS. Distinguished pilot and leader. Arrived with Cullerton for D-Day operations. Achieved Double Ace Status (6.0 Aerial; 6.0 Ground).

Jameson, Bill

Bill Cullerton's maternal grandfather. An avid outdoorsman, Bill Jameson, owned the Jameson Fishing Lure Co. of Chicago and invented the "twin spin" lure. He taught Bill about the outdoors in the Northwoods area of Wisconsin and secured jobs as a hunting and fiching guide for young Cullerton. These skills would later help save Bill's life in Germany.

Kelly, Edward

Mayor of Chicago during World War II.

Kinnard, Claiborne Jr.

Colonel USAAF; HQ of 355th Fighter Group. Distinguished pilot; leader of the 355th Fighter Group, both active and administrative. Achieved Multiple Ace Status (8.0 Aerial; 17.0 Ground). Second-highest score in the 355th Fighter Group. A pilot mentor to Bill.

Lutheran Nuns

Nuns pressed into service at Feuchtwangen Hospital under threat of death by German military. The sisters assumed all nursing duties at the hospital and they were protected by Dr. Maier and his staff. The sisters brought food to Cullerton at the risk of death.

Maier, Dr. Arthur

German-Jewish doctor, originally from Munich, Germany, who was in charge of Feuchtwangen Hospital in Germany. Protected Cullerton from German Military. Facilitated Cullerton's last escape at great personal risk. Maier survived the war.

Marshall, Bert Jr.

Captain USAAF 354th FS. Very distinguished pilot. Excellent leader. Achieved Double Ace Status (7.0 Aerial; 4.0 Ground).

Minchew, Leslie

Captain USAAF 357th FS. Mentored Cullerton when Cullerton first joined the 357th FS. Achieved Ace Status (5.5 Air; .5 Ground).

Priest, Royce

Lieutenant USAAF 354th FS. Landed P-51 behind German lines to rescue Bert Marshall, who landed a disabled aircraft in a risky maneuver. They both escaped. Achieved Ace Status (5 Air)

Riggs, John Dix

Lieutenant USAAF 357th FS. Wingman to Cullerton on August 16, 1944. One of Riggs's external fuel tanks did not release during enemy engagement and he lost control of the plane. Killed in Action.

Righetti, Elwyn

Colonel USAAF. The No. 1 Strafing Ace of the US Eighth Air Force. Killed by German civilians, outside of Dresden, after he surrendered on April 17, 1945, during Cullerton's ordeal. Righetti's plane had been damaged and he soft-landed.

Righetti had 27 strafing kills to his credit—seven on the day he was captured and murdered.

Spencer, Harry

Lieutenant USAAF 357th FS. Distinguished pilot and friend of Cullerton's from Chicago. Progressed through training with Cullerton. Spencer just missed Ace Status (2.0 Aerial; 2.0 Ground).

Stephen, Elaine

Bill Cullerton's girlfriend, fiancé, and wife. Elaine "Steve" Stephen was from Oak Park.

Strobel, Erwin

German citizen and body robber who would strip valuables from dead or wounded citizens and military. This character was real.

Washington, Sgt. Jimmy

The black American sergeant in charge of the .50 caliber machine gun, on the tank that rescued Bill, was real.

Military Terms

354th Fighter Squadron
One of the three fighter squadrons that comprised the 355th Fighter Group based at Steeple Morden, England. Their mascot was the English bulldog.

355th Fighter Group
Comprised of three fighter squadrons (354th, 357th, and 358th) and the Second Scout Force. Based at Station 122 in Steeple Morden, England.

357th Fighter Squadron
One of the three fighter squadrons that comprised the 355th Fighter Group based at Steeple Morden, England. Their mascot was a dragon. Cullerton was a member of the 357th.

358th Fighter Squadron
One of the three fighter squadrons that comprised the 355th Fighter Group based at Steeple Morden, England. Their mascot was an angel.

Aerodrome
Refers to a German Luftwaffe airbase.

B-17 Flying Fortress
Boeing-built American heavy long-range bomber aircraft. Considered a fortress because it was heavily armed and able to defend itself better than most other bombers. Crew included: Pilot, Co-Pilot, Navigator, Bombardier (also served as Front Gunner), Top Turret Gunner, Ball (Belly) Gunner, 2 Waist

Gunners, and a Tail Gunner. Armed or not, the bombers flew with a 75 percent casualty rate until the Mustangs arrived.

B-24 Liberator

Boeing-built American heavy long-range bomber. Armed similar to the B-17. High casualty rate like the B-17s, until the Mustangs arrived.

Buzz Bomb

Nickname for the German-built rocket-propelled flying bomb. The V-1 rocket, was the world's first cruise missile. The V-1 was launched from France and targeted to strike London and other British cities during WWII.

Der Werwolf

Unofficial division of the SS activated toward the end of the war. These were Plainclothes soldiers who would commit acts of terror, such as assassination, car bombs, and spying on fellow German citizens suspected of collaboration with the advancing Allies.

Focke-Wulfe 190

Excellent German fighter aircraft. Radial engine. Underrated in the shadow of the legendary Messerschmitt Me 109 German fighter aircraft. By the end of WWII, the Germans extended the nose of the FWs and installed a water-cooled engine. The upgraded FW was faster than the Mustang, but it came too late.

Luftwaffe

The name of the Germain Air Force in WWII. Literally translated as "Air Waves." The Luftwaffe was the most powerful air force in the world until early 1944 when the US Eighth, Ninth and Fifteenth Air Forces began to overwhelm it in both numbers and killing power.

Me 109/bf 109

This was the famous German Messerschmitt fighter airplane of WWII; one of the most lauded fighter airplanes of all time.

Me 262

The first operational jet fighter aircraft in history was built by Messerschmidt. It entered the war too late to be effective for Germany. Top speed of over 500 mph. Armament 20 mm cannon.

P-47 Thunderbolt

Powerful and durable American fighter aircraft used in WWII but with limited range; it could not cover bombers all the way to Germany. Phased out in favor of the P-51 Mustang that could fly to Berlin and back. P-47s were excellent strafer aircraft with superior firepower and ability to endure more ground-fire hits than the Mustang. Armament: eight wing-mounted .50 caliber machine guns.

P-51 Mustang

Fighter aircraft built by North American Aviation. Originally contracted by Great Britain in 1940 to replace the Spitfire. Effectively entered the war in early 1944 and subsequently played a major roll in the destruction of the German war machine. Used primarily for the escort and protection of Allied bombers from enemy aircraft. The P-51D, with the fiberglass bubble canopy, was considered to be the greatest fighter aircraft ever produced. Fastest propeller-driven pursuit aircraft ever built. Only the German Messerschmitt Me 262 jet fighter could outrun the Mustang. Armament: six wing-mounted .50 caliber machine guns. The wing-mounted external drop fuel tanks allowed the Mustang to escort bombers all the way to Berlin and back.

RAF

Britain's Royal Air Force. The RAF was the last line of defense to save Britain from invasion by Germany in 1940, before the United States entered the war. The RAF retained control of the skies of Great Britain and thus thwarted a planned German invasion. That air battle is considered to be one of the most heroic efforts of survival in history, as the RAF was significantly outnumbered by the German Luftwaffe.

Roll

A flight term which describes the plane turning wing over wing and continuing until the pilot is upright. A 360 degree roll.

SS Officer

An officer in the *Schutzstaffel* (German for protection squadron). The SS was a German political paramilitary organization that developed a military (*Waffen*, or arms) branch. The SS did not adhere to the Geneva Convention rules of war.

Snap Roll

A flight term for a defensive or escape maneuver by a fighter being chased by another. By quickly turning upside down, or inverted, and breaking in any direction, a fighter has a better chance of escaping the pursuer.

Strafe/Strafing/Strafer

The aerial military tactic of flying fighter aircraft very close to the ground and firing guns or dropping bombs strategically, with the sole purpose of destroying the enemy, airplanes, airports, railroad marshalling yards, vehicles, ships, and personnel.

USAAF

United States Army Air Force. In WWII the US Air Force was still part of the US Army.

Captain William J. Cullerton's Commendations and Awards

Bill Cullerton received the following awards or decorations for his military contribution during the war:

The Distinguished Service Cross

(For distinguished service on 11/24/44 in shooting down two enemy fighters in the air and destroying six more on the ground, for a total of eight in one day. This was a first for the US Eighth Air Force.)

The Silver Star

(For destroying seven enemy aircraft on the ground, on 9/12/44. This was a first for the US Eighth Air Force.)

The Distinguished Flying Cross (with three clusters)

(For distinguished service in combat situation on several occasions. For achieving Aerial Ace status.)

The Air Medal (with seven clusters)

(For distinguished service in aerial tactics during service, including extraordinary strafing accomplishments.)

The Purple Heart

(For wounds received in combat. Specifically, the near-fatal gunshot wound received from the SS in April 1945.)

The Presidential Unit Citation

(For being a contributing number of the 355th FG, which claimed the most ground kills in the US Eighth Air Force and was the third-highest-ranking Fighter Group in the US Eighth Air Force.)

The Warsaw Uprising Cross

(For flying fighter cover for the bombers who delivered supplies to the Polish resistance in the Warsaw uprising of 1944.)

CPSIA information can be obtained at www.ICGtesting.com
Printed in the USA
LVOW100550241112

308435LV00002B/4/P